LEADERS
AND
LEADERSHIP

LEADERS
AND
LEADERSHIP

*An Appraisal of Theory
and Research*

MOSTAFA REJAI
AND KAY PHILLIPS

PRAEGER

Westport, Connecticut
London

Library of Congress Cataloging-in-Publication Data

Rejai, M. (Mostafa)
    Leaders and leadership : an appraisal of theory and research /
Mostafa Rejai and Kay Phillips.
        p. cm.
    Includes bibliographical references and index.
    ISBN 0–275–95880–9 (alk. paper)
    1. Leadership. I. Phillips, Kay. II. Title.
HM146.R436 1997
    303.3′4—dc21   96–53942

British Library Cataloguing in Publication Data is available.

Library of Congress Catalog Card Number: 96–53942
ISBN: 0–275–95880–9

First published in 1997

Praeger Publishers, 88 Post Road West, Westport, CT 06881
An imprint of Greenwood Publishing Group, Inc.

Printed in the United States of America

The paper used in this book complies with the
Permanent Paper Standard issued by the National
Information Standards Organization (Z39.48–1984).

10 9 8 7 6 5 4 3 2 1

In Memorium

THOMAS PAUL JENKIN

(University of California, Los Angeles)

Contents

Preface

This book has three interrelated objectives. First, it covers a wide range of topics on leaders and leadership. Second, it presents up-to-date treatments of the subjects it covers—as up to date as the extant literature allows. Third, it offers an extensive bibliography for further study and research.

Chapter 1 attempts to come to grips with the slippery task of defining leadership. Chapter 2 discusses not only the relationship between leaders and followers but also the skills leaders need in order to perform their tasks. Chapter 3 adapts James MacGregor Burns's typology of leaders by looking at transforming leaders (charismatic, revolutionary, and entrepreneurial); transactional leaders (loyalist, symbolic, and manufactured); and military leaders, who, depending on circumstances, may be either transforming or transactional.

Chapter 4 tackles the elusive subject of motivations of leaders by examining the psychoanalytic, psychohistorical, empirical, and experimental approaches. Chapter 5 focuses on the functions of leaders: moral purpose, national unity, system functions, human needs, personal needs, and evolutionary functions.

Chapter 6 examines two types of comparative studies of

leaders: cross-temporal and cross-national. Chapter 7 considers the neglected subject of women leaders at the transnational, national, and subnational levels. Chapter 8 concludes the volume by highlighting some research frontiers in the study of leaders and leadership.

Organized on a chapter-by-chapter basis, the bibliography serves as a comprehensive reference source and as an opportunity for further study and research.

We have tried to keep the book as broad and general as possible. However, our professional background in political science, psychology, sociology, and anthropology unavoidably has affected our choice of topics and the manner in which we treat them.

Offered as a professional contribution, the volume is also well suited for use in courses on leaders and leadership at all levels of college and university curriculums.

Acknowledgments

This book traces its genesis to two sources: (1) a graduate seminar the first author taught for many years at Miami University, and (2) our ongoing research into leaders and leadership over the past two and a half decades. We are grateful to our graduate students and to a large number of research assistants for intellectual stimulation and logistical support.

Among Miami University librarians particularly resourceful at locating research materials, we note Sarah Barr, Penny Beile, Jennifer Block, John Diller, Rebecca Morgenson, Jenny Presnell, and Scott Van Dam.

Some of the research reported in this book was conducted at the Center for International Affairs, Harvard University, and the Hoover Institution, Stanford University. We are grateful to the officers and staffs of these organizations for superbly productive opportunities.

Miami University has supported our work in every conceivable way through the years. Betty Marak "processed" successive drafts of the manuscript with exemplary expertise and good humor.

John Dan Eades of Praeger Publishers remains a source of inspiration. Joanne Freeman did a superb job of copyediting. Claire Cropper, Diane T. Spalding, and Karen

Treat skillfully steered the manuscript through production. We alone remain responsible for any errors of fact or interpretation in connection with this work.

LEADERS
AND
LEADERSHIP

CHAPTER 1

Concepts of Leadership

APPROACHES TO DEFINITION

Leadership has been a central concern of social and political theory since time immemorial. Yet, as Burns (1978, 2) noted, the subject remains "one of the most observed and least understood phenomena on earth." In fact, as of this writing, no universally accepted definition or conception of leadership has emerged.

Some of the earliest writers approached leadership in terms of the "Great Man" and his traits. Among this group, the following are particularly noteworthy: Plato and the Philosopher King, Niccolò Machiavelli and the Prince, Thomas Carlyle and the Hero, Friedrich Nietzsche and the Superman. (For expedient excerpts from the individuals mentioned in this and the following two paragraphs, see Kellerman 1986.)

A second group of theorists dismissed the ideas of leadership traits and the Great Man, stressing instead the role of situations and social forces. Among this group, the following stand out: Adam Smith and the Invisible Hand, Herbert Spencer and Social Darwinism, Karl Marx and the Class Struggle.

A third group of scholars sought to synthesize the trait and the situational schools. As early as 1880, William James stressed the need to create a fit between the "man" and the "hour." The definitive benchmark study fusing the two schools was undertaken by Ralph M. Stogdill ([1948] 1974). Since that time, virtually all studies of leadership recognize the interaction of traits and situations.

Thus, Gibb (1958, 1969) developed an interactional theory stressing the interplay of the leader, the followers, the situation, and the goal. Fiedler (1964) elaborated the interactional perspective into a contingency model, arguing that leadership is dependent on two variables: the leader's goal structure (task orientation vs. relationship orientation) and the situational controls that enable the leader to influence the outcome of group activities.

As a variant of the contingency model, House (1971) formulated a "path-goal theory," maintaining that pursuit of organizational objectives is enhanced when the leader directs the followers to paths that are rewarding to both the followers and the organization. Fiedler subsequently (Fiedler and Garcia 1987) revised his formulation by conjoining the contingency model with "cognitive resource theory," the latter consisting of the leader's intellectual abilities, technical competence, and task-relevant experience.

Hollander (Hollander and Julian 1968; Hollander 1978) developed a transactional theory by combining the situational approach with a social exchange component that focused on reciprocal influences (give and take) between the leader and the followers.

Paige (1972) proclaimed political leadership "an emerging field" and called for systematic studies of the subject on a global scale. Burns (1978), one of the most influential scholars in recent years, stressed several aspects of leadership. First, Burns maintained, leadership is dissensual in that it is rooted in conflict and power over the authoritative allocation of values for a society. Second, leadership is collective in that it involves leader-follower interaction. Third, leadership is purposeful and causative in that it leads to the creation of ideas, movements, institutions, nations. Fourth, leadership takes two forms depending on the goals involved. Transactional leadership consists of exchanges between leaders and followers toward meeting mutual needs and wants (e.g., exchange of jobs for votes); it aims at such "modal values" as fairness, honesty, and responsibility. Transforming leadership, in addition to addressing exchanges of mutual needs, exacts sacrifice from followers; it is morally elevating and aims at such "end-values" as liberty, equality, and justice.

Tucker (1981) equated all politics with leadership, insisting, moreover, that any approach to leadership must be value neutral, to enable us to study such monster-leaders as Stalin and Hitler. Departing sharply from the foregoing approaches, Bailey (1988) pointedly titled his book *Humbuggery and Manipulation: The Art of Leadership*.

Taking his inspiration from Burns, criticizing "the industrial leadership paradigm," and calling for a "postindustrial" conception of leadership, Rost (1993) offers the following definition: "Leadership is an influence relationship among leader and followers who intend real changes that reflect their mutual purposes" (102; original in italics). While this conception—as well as that of Burns—accommodates democratic forms of leadership, it is manifestly inconsistent with the authoritarian, dictatorial, and totalitarian varieties.

Heifetz (Heifetz and Sindler 1987; Heifetz 1994) has recently reconceptualized leadership as the mobilization of group resources toward solving group problems and achieving group objectives. He views leadership as primarily *adaptive* in nature. In addition, he stresses the concept of *authority* (legitimate power) as inseparable from leadership, while acknowledging that in some circumstances (for instance, dictatorships or leaders without formal office, e.g., Martin Luther King, Jr.) it is possible to "lead" without authority.

Rejai and Phillips (1979, 1983, 1988, 1996) developed an interactional theory for the study of political and military leaders, stressing the interplay between sociodemographic variables, psychological dynamics, and situational forces. While this theory was satisfactory for the authors' limited purposes, by no means did it yield a unified conception of leadership. Rather than focusing on leadership as such, Rejai and Phillips were primarily interested in two questions: who leaders are and how they emerge upon the scene.

Leadership and Power

Virtually all conceptions of leadership embody—implicitly or explicitly—a concept of power, typically defined as the ability to influence the behavior of others. Indeed, one scholar (Janda 1960) approached leadership *exclusively* in terms of power.

Burns (1978) maintains that leadership is different from mere power holding or brute force. Leadership is authority or legitimate power in that it involves "mutual persuasion, exchange, elevation, and transformation" (1978, 11).

According to Burns, the two essentials of power are motives and resources. Motives are the purposes or the goals of both power holders and power recipients; they are collective and relational. Resources constitute the wants and needs of both power holders and power recipients. Hence, the power process involves three elements: "the motives and resources of power holders; the motives and resources of power recipients; and the relationships among all these" (1978, 13). Returning to his theme of moral transformation, Burns concludes: "Like power, leadership is relational, collective, and purposeful. Leadership shares with power the central function of achieving purpose" (1978, 18).

While Burns's conceptions of leadership and power have a Western democratic bias, French and Raven (1959) offer a more neutral approach. They define power in terms of influence and the production of change in the behavior, attitude, goal, value, need, and so forth, of power recipients. They maintain that there are many different types of power; each type has different roots, produces different changes, and yields different consequences.

More specific, French and Raven argue that there are five bases of social power, each producing a different form of power: (1) reward power is based on the power recipient's perception that the power holder has the ability to produce reward; (2) coercive power is based on the power recipient's perception that the power holder can produce punishment; (3) legitimate power is based on the power recipient's perception that the power holder has a sanctioned right (as in an election) to prescribe behavior; (4) referent power is based on the power recipient's identification with the power holder; and (5) expert power is based on the power recipient's perception that the power holder has special knowledge.

These five types of power, according to French and Raven, are interdependent and overlapping, seldom existing in isolation. Moreover they maintain that the stronger the power base, the stronger the power (e.g., the power of reward power will vary with the importance of the reward); and the stronger the power recipient's perception of the power base, the stronger the power.

In short, all leadership involves power—from the gentlest persuasion to the brutest force.

Leadership and Management

Leadership and management are frequently fused and confused, but they are not one and the same thing. In a classic article, Zaleznik (1977) maintained that leaders and managers represent different personality types, develop in different ways, have different values and orientations, and meet different needs and functions. Specifically, leaders have visions, think and behave in intuitive ways, and are drawn to disorder; managers are tinkerers, problem solvers, and are driven by rationality and efficiency. Leaders and managers, Zaleznik argued, differ in: (1) their *attitude toward goals* (leaders shape new goals and objectives; managers administer and supervise the status quo), (2) their *conception of work* (leaders view work as risk-taking opportunities; managers are driven by compromise, bargaining, and negotiations), (3) their *relations with others* (leaders show and generate emotions; managers treat people as things), and (4) their *sense of self* (leaders are "twice-born" and experience discontinuities in life; managers are "once-born" and experience routine socialization and adjustments).

In more recent times Rost (1993) defined management in the following terms: "Management is an authority relationship between at least one manager and one subordinate who coordinate their activities to produce and sell particular goods and/or services" (145; original in italics). Recalling his definition of leadership discussed earlier, it follows that (1) leadership is an influence relationship, whereas management is an authority relationship; (2) leadership involves leaders and followers, whereas management deals with managers and subordinates;

(3) leadership seeks profound changes, whereas management focuses on production and sale of goods and/or services; (4) in leadership intended changes reflect mutual purposes, whereas in management goods and services result from coordinated superior and subordinate activities (Rost, 1993, 148–52).

THE ENIGMA OF LEADERSHIP

Bailey notwithstanding, the foregoing theories have helped us clarify traits, situations, contingencies, interactions, transactions, transformations, and the like. Cumulatively, moreover, these theories have provided us with a rich and variegated literature for intellectual nourishment and discourse.

Why is it, then, as Bennis (1959), Burns (1978), Bennis and Nanus (1985), and others have pointed out, that leadership is among the most studied and least understood subjects on earth? Why is it that in one way or another most writers express uneasiness with the subject? Why is it that some scholars find it necessary to dwell on the "ambiguity" of leadership (e.g., Pfeffer 1978) or the "romance" of leadership (e.g, Meindl, Ehrich, and Eukerich 1985)? Why is it that others (e.g., see McCall and Lombardo 1978) speak of leadership variously as "docility," a "language game," a "high performing system," and the like? Why is it that some writers (e.g., see McCall 1977) have called for abandoning the concept altogether?

The reasons, we suggest, are two. First, leadership has attracted scholars from a variety of disciplines who bring contrasting perspectives to the subject: political science, sociology, anthropology, psychology, philosophy, management, education. Second, a pivotal dimension of leadership remains unaddressed in the extant literature. Specifically, while students of leadership have uniformly stressed the centrality of leader-follower interaction, very little of substance has been said about the *nature* or *dynamics* of that interaction. *Why* do followers respond as they do? Elemental in character, this overlooked dimension, we maintain, has rendered the subject of leadership enigmatic (cf. Wills 1994).[1]

Having identified the enigma of leadership, we face a number of serious problems, some of them perhaps insurmountable. Difficult as psychological studies of leaders have been,[2] investigation of follower psychologies promises to tax the energy and imagination of even the most enthusiastic researchers. How does one identify followers? How does one isolate them for study? How does one collect data about them? How does one study follower motivation and psychology? What methodological operations does one adopt? What interpretive guidelines does one employ?

Nonetheless, if we are to accept the proposition that leadership is a leader-follower interaction, then only systematic studies of follower personalities can shed light on the enigma of leadership. Perhaps we will learn that leadership is not any *one* "thing" or relationship or process. Perhaps there are as many leadership styles as there are types of follower responses. Perhaps there are as many leadership theories as there are leadership styles. Perhaps in any universal sense leadership is unknowable.

To be sure, some writers (e.g., Le Bon 1908; Freud [1921] 1960) have undertaken speculative studies of follower psychologies, typically in terms of irrational and pathological behavior. A few others (e.g., Rudé 1959, 1964; Hoerder 1977) have engaged in empirical investigations of the political and economic mainsprings of follower behavior. (See Chapter 2.) However, most such studies have addressed the issue of why people become involved in social *movements*, not why they follow specific *leaders*.[3] Actual studies of follower psychology and motivation constitute a field yet to be charted and cultivated. Meanwhile, perhaps we should be satisfied with the meager literature currently at our disposal.

SUMMARY

Given the many difficulties enunciated in the foregoing pages, we offer the following working conception of leadership as satisfactory for purposes of study and research.

Leadership refers to life experiences and life chances that (1) imbue a person with a vision and a set of goals, (2) endow that person with the skill to articulate the vision and the goals in such a way as to attract a significant following, (3) provide that person with the skill to specify the means and to organize and mobilize the followers toward the realization of the vision and the goals, and (4) give that person sufficient understanding of the followers in order to devise and pursue goals that are rewarding to both the leader and the followers.

This conception has certain advantages over other conceptions. First, it is synthetic in that it draws upon the strong points of the definitions we have considered. Second, it is value-neutral in that it applies to all leadership situations—North and South, East and West, democratic and dictatorial. Third and related, it is inclusive in that it accommodates Moses as well as Mussolini, Gandhi as well as Stalin, Mother Teresa as well as Adolf Hitler, Jesse Jackson as well as Oliver North. Finally, it helps settle a long-standing controversy in leadership studies: leaders are not *born*; they are *made*.

We now turn to a more detailed examination of some of the salient issues raised in this chapter.

NOTES

1.   Not wishing to claim immunity to this oversight, we should acknowledge that in a series of studies (Rejai and Phillips 1979, 1983, 1988, 1996), we had no alternative but simply to assume that certain historic figures in fact acted as leaders, and then to proceed to analyze their characteristics and traits. We had no logical way of exploring leader-follower interaction in the historical contexts which we investigated.

2.   Among such studies we include Barber (1965), George (1968), Gurr (1970), Hermann (1977), Iremonger (1970), Lasswell (1930 [1960]), Payne et al. (1984), Rejai and Phillips (1988), Winter (1973), and the sources cited therein. By no means do we suggest that these studies have settled the issue of leader psychology, only that they have addressed it. See also Chapter 4.

3.   Major exceptions are Abel's ([1938] 1965) analysis of the "adherents of the Hitler movement" and Willner's (1984) discussion of "charismatic leaders."

CHAPTER 2

Leaders, Followers, and Skills

Following up on the concepts just discussed, in this chapter we consider three interrelated questions about leaders and followers: (1) Who are followers? (2) Why do followers follow? (3) How do leaders lead?

WHO ARE FOLLOWERS?

Studies of followers have taken two forms: speculative and empirical. Among the former we include Le Bon (1908, 1913) and Freud ([1921] 1960); among the latter, Brinton (1930), Rudé (1959), Hoerder (1977), and Abel (1938). These studies will be presented in the sequential order of the topics or events they cover.

Speculative Studies

Speculative studies are not data based; they are pejorative, negative, and condemnatory. Le Bon's 1908 book, *The Crowd*, was influenced by Freud and his emphasis on the role of the unconscious and the irrational in human affairs. In turn, the book became a pacesetter, influencing many writers who followed, including Sigmund Freud himself.

The very title of Le Bon's book carries a negative connotation. The French title *La foule* is translated variously as crowd, throng, multitude, or mob. The verb *fouler* means to trample down or to tread upon.

Le Bon speaks of the "law of mental unity of crowds," meaning that a number of individuals coming together to form a crowd take on new characteristics quite separate from their own. Specifically, the crowd develops a "collective mind" in which the unconscious reigns supreme, irrationality and emotionality are heightened, instincts take over, destructiveness sets in, and individuals act as mindless creatures. Crowd behavior is contagious to such a degree that an individual sacrifices his personal interest to the collective interest. Other characteristics of crowds are impulsiveness, irritability, and intolerance.

The crowd has an "instinctive need" for leadership; it cannot do without a master. Crowd *leaders* are deranged persons bordering on insanity and madness. Crowd *members* are degenerates, thieves, beggars, and assassins. As such, crowds are "barbarians" and "savages"; they represent the "triumph of atavistic instincts." (For a parallel argument, see Hoffer 1958.)

In *Group Psychology and the Analysis of the Ego* ([1921] 1960), Freud agrees with Le Bon that group behavior is characterized by regressiveness, irrationality, emotionality, unpredictability, and anarchy. However, whereas Le Bon had attributed group dynamics primarily to contagion, Freud introduces the dimension of leadership as the key to understanding collective phenomena:

[A] group is . . . as intolerant as it is obedient to authority. It respects force and can only be slightly influenced by kindness, which it regards merely as a form of weakness. What it demands of its heroes is strength, or even violence. It wants to be ruled and oppressed and to fear its masters. (Freud 1921, 14)

The mutual ties that bind group members are based upon their common libidinal/emotional (but desexualized) ties to the leader. This, according to Freud, is "the essence of group mind," determining its cohesiveness and unity. The followers' common identification with the leader shapes their mode of identification toward one another as well.

The followers' emotional ties to the leader stem from persistent tension within their personalities. Specifically, within their psychic apparatus, the ego (the rationality principle) is too weak to resolve the eternal conflict between the id (instinctual forces) and the superego (social/moral imperatives). Since the followers are unable to measure up to their own "ego ideal" (as represented by the superego), they look to the leader, who represents the group's ego ideal. Accordingly, the group wishes to be governed by "unrestricted force"; it has "a passion for authority."

Empirical Studies

Brinton (1930) studied some 17,400 members of Jacobin clubs throughout France for the revolutionary period 1789–1795. The Jacobins constituted the most radical element in the French Revolution. Brinton's sources were documents of various Jacobin clubs plus French tax rolls for the period in question. His findings directly contradict all the basic assumptions of the speculative studies.

The mean age of the Jacobins was forty-two. As for socioeconomic status, 60 percent were middle class, 30 percent working class, and 10 percent peasants. The occupations of the Jacobins were consistent with their largely middle class status: lawyers, priests, teachers, artists, businessmen, civil servants. This finding was confirmed by the investigation of the tax rolls: being relatively well off, the Jacobins paid higher taxes than the average population. Accordingly, Brinton concluded, the Jacobins were neither nobles nor beggars. Except for lack of representation from the upper class, they represented a cross section of their communities.

Rudé's *The Crowd in the French Revolution* (1959) expanded and elaborated on Brinton's study. For his data Rudé relied on police records of the National Archives and of the Paris Prefecture of Police for the period 1787–1795. He sought to answer two questions: (1) Who were the persons that turned out in the streets of Paris? (2) What was their motivation?

As for the first question, Rudé found that, in addition to the sans-culottes, the French Revolution attracted primarily middle and lower class individuals. Among middle class citizens were owners, landlords, merchants, civil servants, shopkeepers, teachers, lawyers, and priests. Among lower class persons were wage earners, journeymen, metal workers, dressmakers, cabinet makers, shoemakers, builders, engravers, cooks, waiters, tailors, hairdressers, porters, and domestic servants.

As for the second question, Rudé stressed the interplay of political and economic forces. On the political side was the attraction of the ideas embodied in the Declaration of the Rights of Man and Citizen—and of Liberty, Equality, Fraternity—all representing the revolt of the middle and lower classes against the ancient regime. On the economic side were the people's demands for the daily necessities of life, especially food, as "the primary and most constant" motive of the revolutionaries.

Revolutionary crowds, Rudé concluded, far from being social abstractions, were composed of ordinary men and women moved by the attraction of new political ideas and by the pressures of economic necessity.

Rudé's data are necessarily biased in that they were limited to persons who had been arrested or imprisoned. But the point is precisely that even the most active and radical segments of the population are "normal," and that, in contrast to the speculative studies, crowd action is rational and understandable.

Hoerder's *Crowd Action in Revolutionary Massachusetts* (1977) focuses on the period 1765–1780 and does for the American Revolution what Rudé had done for the French. Hoerder's data sources are available tax lists, court records, official documents, newspapers, private papers, diaries, and the like.

Hoerder's findings are consistent with Rudé's. As for the *who* question, Hoerder finds crowd action involved merchants, artisans, laborers, farmers, landlords, owners, lawyers, teachers, priests, and politicians. As for the *why* question, we come once again upon the interplay of political and economic forces. A virtually endless list of popular grievances relative to British acts, duties, and taxes generated a series of crowd actions that began in the urban centers and spread to the rural areas. Liberty, property, and natural rights were the issues for which most everyone stood up. The unifying factor, however, was taxation: since no colonials were left untouched by taxes, resistance was general.

Hoerder goes one step beyond Rudé by arguing that in the American case crowd action was essentially defensive and conservative: it sought restoration of the past, a tradition having roots in the ideas of natural law and natural rights.

Abel ([1938] 1965) set out to identify the followers of the Hitler movement. During a visit to Germany in 1933, he announced a monetary prize contest inviting Nazi party members and sympathizers to submit personal histories, including age, family background, education, occupation, socioeconomic status, and reasons for joining the Hitler movement. Abel received 683 responses, of which 600 proved usable. He found:

> By taking the modal values of these data, we arrive at the following fictitious average type of follower of the Hitler movement: He is male, in his early thirties, a town resident of lower middle-class origin, without high school education; married and Protestant; participated in the World War, but not in the military activities during the revolution of 1918 or later outbreaks; had no political affiliations before joining the National Socialist party and belonged to no veteran or semi-military organizations. He joined the party between 1930 and 1931, and had his first contacts with the movement through readings about it and attending a meeting. He was strongly dissatisfied with the republican regime in Germany, but had no specific anti-Semitic bias. His economic status was secure, for not once did he have to change his occupation, job, or residence, nor was he ever unemployed. (Abel [1938] 1965, 6)

As for the question of motivation, generally speaking, the appeal of the Nazis derived directly from the well-known triple crises of the Weimar Republic: the political crisis (fragmentation, struggle, and lack of effective leadership), the economic crisis (inflation and unemployment), and the psychological crisis (the aftermath of defeat in World War I).

WHY DO FOLLOWERS FOLLOW?

This question has been approached in a variety of ways, and in this section we shall examine some of the more prominent studies.

Adorno and his associates (1951) were concerned with the identification of the "potentially fascist" personality. They hypothesized that the social and political convictions of the individual form a coherent pattern, and that this pattern is a reflection of deep-lying personality traits.

The approach is Freudian, stressing the inner workings of the mind—particularly the interplay between the id (instinctual forces), the superego (morality principle), and the ego (rationality principle). In a "normal" personality these three dynamics are characterized by balance and harmony. In an "authoritarian" personality, there is system dysfunction.

On a theoretical level, the "authoritarian syndrome" follows a distinct pattern. The superego has become overly strong and punitive (possibly as a response to overly strict parents), trying to deny gratification to the id. The stronger the superego, the more rebellious the id in search of instinctual gratification. The stronger the superego-id conflict, the weaker the ego in performing its mediating function. The result is a system breakdown.

The chief behavioral manifestations of the authoritarian personality are four. First, the individual is closed-minded, conformist, and entirely lacking in empathy. Second, having low self-esteem, the individual is obsessed by fears of being weak; he becomes highly compulsive and ritualistic, and he identifies with people of high status. Third, the individual exhibits highly ambivalent tendencies, particularly sadomasochism and manic-depression. Finally, the individual is authoritarian and submissive at the same time—authoritarian and violent vis-à-vis those he considers inferior, submissive and deferential toward those he considers superior.

Adorno and his associates concluded that such a personality is susceptible to totalitarian movements, and that totalitarian movements are capable of manipulating the behavioral tendencies of the "authoritarian personality" by promising power and security.

The Adorno study has been faulted for using Freudian theory, which, as we have said before, is nonempirical and nonscientific. However, other studies have found that the three recurring traits of authoritarianism are submissiveness, aggression, and conformity.

The Adorno study has also been faulted for lack of attention to social, cultural, and economic variables. This criticism has been addressed by Fromm (1941), who observes that in times past we lived in small communities characterized by intimate, face-to-face relations. The family, the church, and the community gave us security but at the same time limited our freedom. Modern, mass industrial society shattered this order of life. We have been freed from the bonds of family, church, and community, but we have not gained real freedom. (Fromm distinguishes between "positive freedom" or "freedom to," meaning ability to do things, and "negative freedom" or "freedom from," meaning absence of restraint.)

In short, past communities were high on security and low on freedom while modern societies are low on security and low on positive freedom. As a result, we have become isolated, alienated, uprooted, impotent, and powerless. As this situation becomes unbearable, we escape from (negative) freedom into submission, dependency, compulsive and irrational behavior. That is to say, we seek what we have lost: security, belongingness, community. And we do so by automaton conformity or by destructiveness or by joining authoritarian movements.

Other scholars take a somewhat different approach: they argue that under modern conditions individuals often have no choice *but* to follow. In a classic study ([1915] 1962), Michels maintains that democracy and self-rule are impossible and undesirable because human beings are irrational and incapable of self-rule. Every society is characterized by a division between the few who rule and the many who are ruled.

Indeed, Michels applies the principle of minority rule not only to societies but to organizations of whatever origin, intent, and size. Organizations may begin as democracies, Michels argues, but the rise of oligarchy is unavoidable. (Michels's specific focus is the German Social Democratic Party, the implication being that if a social democratic party becomes oligarchical, one can only imagine the fate of conservative and authoritarian parties.)

The reasons for the rise of oligarchy, according to Michels, are that the leaders are always in a position to structure or restructure the organization; they monopolize the expertise, the funds, the information, and the incentive system; they control the agenda—which is to say, they control what topics are discussed and not discussed. By contrast, the followers are incompetent and driven by irrational impulses. They have a psychological *need* for leadership. They submit to those who make decisions for them, simplify their lives, and give them order and security. Michels concludes that the Iron Law of Oligarchy is unavoidable and inevitable: "Who says organization, says oligarchy." The followers have no choice in the matter.

Janis's *Groupthink* (1982) argues that even within small groups there are built-in psychological dynamics having homogenizing effects. The aim of the small group is consensus around the views of the principal leader(s), together with suppression of divergent approaches and alternative courses of action. Janis discusses several situations—the Bay of Pigs, the Cuban Missile Crisis, Vietnam, Watergate—to document that groupthink produces inferior policy because the participants are too concerned with losing status or too fearful of rocking the boat to engage in serious discussion of policy alternatives.

"According to the groupthink hypothesis, members of any small cohesive group tend to maintain esprit de corps by unconsciously developing a number of shared illusions and related norms that interfere with critical thinking and reality testing" (Janis 1982, 35). Specifically, in time the group develops an illusion of invulnerability, an illusion of unanimity, an urge to suppress minority views (by "self-appointed mindguards"), and the like. Once again, the "followers" have no choice but to follow.

Milgram (1974) devised an ingenious (though unethical) experiment to show that people are anxious to follow authority figures, even if it means administering cruel and unusual punishment upon their fellow human beings. In Milgram's exercise, subjects were put in the role of "teachers" and were told by the experimenter (wearing a white jacket, symbolizing authority) that the experiment was a study of the effects of punishment on learning. Each "teacher" was positioned at an instrument panel which he thought was capable of administering electric shock to the "learner," who in reality was an actor pretending to be receiving shocks.

The instrument panel consisted of thirty switches ranging in labeled intensity from 15 volts to 450 volts, and in labeled severity from "Slight Shock" to "Danger—Severe Shock." The teacher was to test the learner, shocking the learner with increasing intensity when the learner answered incorrectly. The learner expressed increasing levels of discomfort as the supposed severity of the shocks increased.

Milgram found that every teacher agreed to begin the experiment, and that two-thirds continued to the highest voltage level. Some teachers protested to the experimenter but continued to administer the shocks. Distanced from responsibility for their actions (acting under "orders" from the experimenter, though the experimenter had no means of coercion), the teachers were capable of extraordinary cruelty. Some teachers rationalized their cruelty by stating that stupid people deserved to be shocked. Charged with unethical and deceptive behavior, Milgram responded that truthful circumstances would have yielded inaccurate results.

Zimbardo (1973) experimented with a mock prison in order to study the effects of imprisonment on human behavior. His subjects were ten "prisoners" and eleven "guards," determined by the flip of a coin, chosen for emotional stability and maturity from a pool of seventy-five volunteers. The two groups were outfitted in distinctive and identifiable garbs.

Zimbardo found that within a day guards began to act as guards, and prisoners as prisoners. Specifically, the guards became domineering, overbearing, arbitrary, and sadistic, while the prisoners became dependent, submissive, and childlike. Those who survived the experiment were typically authoritarian personalities. The situation became so fraught with danger that the two-week experiment was aborted after only six days.

The experiment documented the impact of environment on human personality. It also showed that human beings have the potential to be leaders or followers depending on the circumstances.

HOW DO LEADERS LEAD?

The most comprehensive study of leadership strategies is Bennis and Nanus, *Leaders: Strategies for Taking*

Charge (1985). Based on interviews with ninety CEOs, the authors identified four components of leadership strategies:

1. Leaders have visions, goals, programs, agendas.

2. Leaders have the skill to communicate their visions, goals, programs, and agendas and to create shared meaning.

3. Leaders have the ability to generate trust among followers. Important in leader-follower interaction are reciprocal reliability, predictability, and constancy. The component of trust makes possible maintaining organizational integrity, "staying the course," and implementing leader vision.

4. Leaders have the ability to develop the self through two elements:

   a. having positive self-regard; recognizing one's strengths and weaknesses; nurturing skills and discipline; seeing the fit between one's skills and the tasks to be performed.

   b. avoiding the Wallenda factor; not fearing failure; learning from failure and moving forward; concentrating on winning, not losing. (Wallenda, the high-wire artist, failed—he fell to his death—when he became obsessed with fear of failure.)

Through these four strategies, leaders empower followers to translate intention (vision) into reality and sustain it. Empowerment means that leaders use organizations as means of allowing followers to channel their energies and skills in such a way as to draw satisfaction from what they do. Organizations should be designed to stress competence, community, and enjoyment of work.

In more general terms, we may note that leaders lead by deploying ideology and organization. Ideology is a set of shared beliefs, values, sentiments, and commitments. Organization provides rationality, efficiency, and division of labor; it is a means for implementing ideology. Ideology creates an emotional bond among a group of people; organization creates a rational bond. Together, ideology and organization mobilize the followers toward the realization of visions, values, goals, and objectives.

SUMMARY

In this chapter we have raised three sets of questions about leaders and followers:

1. Who are followers? Speculative studies suggest that followers ("crowds") consist of riffraff and rabble, unstable persons with emotional and psychological problems, irrational and destructive hordes driven by contagion and beguiled by deranged leaders. Empirical studies find that followers are normal men and women from the middle and lower classes driven by political ideals and by the economic necessities of life; crowd action, they conclude, is rational and understandable.

2. Why do followers follow? Because they are authoritarian personalities. Because of a need for security and community in the face of increasing social complexity. Because under modern conditions individuals often have no choice *but* to follow. Because the rise of oligarchy is inevitable. Because groupthink stands in the way of critical thinking and reality testing. Because human beings are conditioned to follow authority figures or to respond to environmental stimuli.

3. How do leaders lead? Using ideology and organization, leaders have the skills to mobilize the followers toward the realization of shared visions, goals, and objectives.

CHAPTER 3

Types of Leaders

Lacking a universally agreed upon definition of leadership (see Chapter 1), we are not in a position to construct a definitive typology of leaders, since the latter task depends upon the former. Accordingly, consistent with the working definition proposed in Chapter 1, we will adapt for our purposes Burns's (1978) distinction between transforming and transactional leaders. Under the former category, we shall include charismatic, revolutionary, and entrepreneurial leaders; under the latter group, we shall incorporate loyalist (establishment), symbolic, and manufactured leaders. We shall cover military leaders under a separate heading, since—given times, circumstances, and personalities—military leaders can be either transforming or transactional.

TRANSFORMING LEADERS

Charismatic Leaders

The term charisma was originally associated with divinely inspired leaders and used in an exclusively religious context. Max Weber (1958, 1964)—with whom the concept of charisma is most prominently associat-

ed—accepted the religious meaning while adding a secular
dimension. He wrote:

> The term "charisma" will be applied to a certain
> quality of an individual personality by virtue of which
> he is set apart from ordinary men and treated as
> endowed with supernatural, superhuman, or at least
> specifically exceptional powers or qualities. These are
> such as are not accessible to ordinary persons, but are
> regarded as of divine origin or as exemplary, and on
> the basis of them the individual concerned is treated as
> a leader. (Weber 1964, 358–59)

To summarize Weber's lengthy formulation, charismatic
leadership has the following characteristics: (1) It is
strictly personal. (2) It refers to exceptional or supernatural
powers. (3) It may be secular or religious. (4) It is a
leader-follower relationship. (5) Its existence requires
voluntary recognition on the part of disciples and followers. (6) This recognition depends upon the demonstration
of constant proof, which, in turn, augments follower
devotion and enthusiasm. (7) Charisma is emotional,
irrational, and communal. (8) It is not bound by rules,
codes, or regulations. (9) It involves a calling or a mission.
(10) It is most likely to emerge in times of crisis. (11) It
is revolutionary and transformative. (12) It is transitory
and subject to routinization.

Weber's conception of charisma set off a controversy of
major proportions in social science literature. Scholars
have variously accepted Weber's formulation, rejected it,
revised it, and applied it to various contexts. A major
effort to emend and apply Weber was undertaken by Ann
Ruth Willner (1984). Charisma, Willner maintains, is a
matter of follower *perceptions*, not leader *qualities*.
Specifically, charismatic leadership is a leader-follower

interaction with the following characteristics: (1) the leader is perceived by the followers as divine or superhuman, (2) the followers unconditionally believe the leader's statements, (3) the followers unconditionally comply with the leader's directives for action, and (4) the followers give the leader unqualified emotional commitment.

Willner proceeds to study the foregoing characteristics in connection with seven leaders: Fidel Castro, Mahatma Gandhi, Adolf Hitler, Ayatollah Khomeini, Benito Mussolini, Franklin Roosevelt, and Ahmed Sukarno. Her evidence consists of uneven and isolated statements and observations about what followers have said about these leaders.

Willner's emendation of Weber must be rated as only marginally successful. For one thing, the seven leaders she studied constitute an unacceptably small sample for social scientific investigation. For another, the problems of studying follower perceptions and reactions in any systematic fashion remain insurmountable.

In general, while the concept of charisma has a certain intuitive appeal, in principle it is not amenable to empirical or scientific analysis and discourse.

Revolutionary Leaders

Rejai and Phillips (1979, 1983) studied 135 revolutionary leaders from thirty-one revolutionary movements in twenty-nine countries across four centuries. They deployed a situational (or interactional) theory of revolutionary leadership, stressing the interplay between sociodemographic variables, psychological dynamics, and situational forces. They gathered uniform data on the 135 revolutionaries with the aim of answering two sets of questions: (1) What are their sociodemographic backgrounds?

(2) What psychological and situational forces propel them toward revolutionary activity?

As for sociodemographic variables, Rejai and Phillips found that revolutionaries are typically in their forties and fifties upon seizing power, although they are exposed to revolutionary ideology—and participate in revolutionary activity—quite early, frequently in their teens. Revolutionaries are either urban-born or, if born and raised in rural areas, they develop early and sustained exposure to urban cultures. Revolutionaries typically enjoy normal and tranquil family lives, even though they have a large number of siblings.

As for socioeconomic status, revolutionaries are 50 percent from the middle class, 30 percent from the lower class, and 20 percent from the upper class. Revolutionaries are mainstream with respect to ethnicity and religion, although in time some of them turn to atheism. Revolutionaries are highly educated, with 75 percent having had college, university, or professional experience. The occupations of revolutionaries are inconsistent with their socioeconomic status and education, in that many become professional revolutionaries. Accordingly, and not surprising, many revolutionaries compile lengthy records of arrest, imprisonment, and exile.

Revolutionaries are highly cosmopolitan, traveling far and wide, gaining exposure to different languages and cultures, and developing a variety of foreign contacts. Revolutionaries are prolific writers, not only on the theory and practice of revolution but on literature, philosophy, and the arts as well. Revolutionaries have a positive view of human nature, an ambivalent view of their own countries (depending on the regime in power), and a dualistic view of international society, distinguishing friends and enemies.

As for psychological findings, eight variables emerged. All revolutionaries are motivated by *nationalism* and by a sense of *justice*: they seek the independence and integrity of their homelands, and they want to right the wrongs they perceive. More than half of the revolutionaries are characterized by *vanity and egotism*. Nearly 75 percent subscribe to an *ascetic, spartan* lifestyle. Nearly half of the revolutionaries are motivated by *relative deprivation, status inconsistency*, or both. (Relative deprivation is the perception of discrepancy between the values one seeks and the values one attains. Status inconsistency is the perception of discrepancy between one's economic status and one's political power.) Over 60 percent of the revolutionaries are *marginal* in some way: they deviate from commonly accepted norms, whether physical, social, or psychological. About half of the revolutionaries exhibit varieties of *estheticism and romanticism*: they are sensitive to things of beauty in art, music, literature, or nature. Only three revolutionaries may have experienced *oedipal complex*: sexual attraction toward the mother, rebelliousness against the father, and history of family conflict and discord.

As for situational variables, Rejai and Phillips identified conditions of national crisis or emergency; colonial contexts (which pit the colonizer against the colonized); the violent histories of such countries as Algeria, China, Colombia, Cuba, Mexico, Palestine, South Africa, and Vietnam; and the role of chance. Also important were such micro-situational variables as birthplace, socioeconomic status, number of siblings, and age ranking among siblings.

Rejai and Phillips concluded that far from being pathological riffraffs, revolutionaries are normal people and revolutionary behavior is rational, understandable, and amenable to empirical investigation and study.

Entrepreneurial Leaders

In *Public Entrepreneurship*, Lewis (1980) studied the lives of three American entrepreneurs: Hyman Rickover, the "father" of the atomic Navy; J. Edgar Hoover, the legendary director of the FBI; and Robert Moses, New York State director of parks and highways. Lewis defined a public entrepreneur as "a person who creates or profoundly elaborates a public organization so as to alter greatly the existing pattern of allocation of public resources" (1980, 9).

Public entrepreneurs arise in organizational contexts that contain contradictory mixes of values from the past, and they proceed to exploit these contradictions. Thus, using the Soviet scare, Admiral Rickover exploited the ambiguity of the role of the military in the Atomic Energy Act of 1946, thereby gaining autonomy from both the Navy and the Atomic Energy Commission. Relying on the crime scare of the 1930s, Hoover created a national police force while at the same time denouncing the idea. And bemoaning the lack of recreational facilities, Moses created "public authorities" for parks and highways by exploiting contradictions and conflicts in New York State politics.

Public entrepreneurs design their organizations in such a way that they simultaneously grant them autonomy and flexibility, minimize external interferences with operations, and appear to be isomorphic with the goals and needs of society. As such, Rickover, Hoover, and Moses made their entrepreneurship appear not only reasonable and necessary, but patriotic as well.

According to Lewis, public entrepreneurship undergoes three stages of development. Stage 1—Early Entrepreneurship—represents the entrepreneur's imperfect and partial socialization to organizational life, together with the attempt, under the guidance of a mentor, to rid the organization of traditions, values, and practices that are deemed inefficient, useless, and irrelevant. Stage 2—The Leap—consists of the act that either creates or elaborates the organization in previously unforeseen ways, together with the attempt to project an apolitical shield to buffer the organization and render it as autonomous as possible. Stage 3—Mature Entrepreneurship—consists of the attempt to make the organization as self-sufficient and self-reliant as possible, to encompass or neutralize competing organizations, and to institutionalize and routinize the organization.

Public entrepreneurs are characterized by expertise, singlemindedness, power orientation, high energy, and hard work. Public entrepreneurial organizations lose their glamour and status as the public entrepreneurs with whom they are identified pass from the scene.

TRANSACTIONAL LEADERS

Loyalist Leaders

Rejai and Phillips (1988) undertook a study of fifty prominent loyalist or establishment leaders from twenty-nine countries spread across four continents and four centuries. Replicating their study of revolutionaries discussed above, once again they deployed an interactional theory of loyalist leadership, stressing the interplay between sociodemographic variables, psychological dynamics, and situational forces. They gathered uniform data on the fifty loyalists with the aim of answering two sets of questions: What are their sociodemographic backgrounds? What psychological and situational forces propel them to loyalist leadership?

As for sociodemographic variables, Rejai and Phillips found that loyalists are typically native-born to legal marriages. They are either urban-born or, if born and raised in rural areas, they develop early and sustained exposure to urban cultures. Although they have a large number of siblings, they tend to be either the oldest or the youngest. They tend to have peaceful, tranquil family lives. They are exposed to political ideology—and participate in political activity—early in life. Their ethnic and religious backgrounds are of the mainstream variety. They are typically from the upper or middle social strata, and their fathers hold prestigious occupations. They are highly educated, frequently in exclusive schools. They are cosmopolitan, traveling far and wide and developing a variety of foreign contacts. They publish on a wide variety of subjects. They have a negative attitude toward human nature, while holding a positive attitude toward their own countries and toward the international community.

As for psychological variables, loyalists uniformly exhibit *patriotism and nationalism*, but very few have a commitment to *social justice*. Some 75 percent of the loyalists are *vain and egotistical*, while fewer than 10 percent are *ascetic and puritanical*. Just under half of the loyalists are motivated by *relative deprivation* and *status inconsistency*. Nearly 75 percent of the loyalists are *marginal* in some way: they markedly differ from standard norms, whether social, psychological, or physical. About a third of the loyalists exhibit some form of *estheticism and romanticism*. Loyalists show no trace of *oedipal problems*.

As for situational variables, loyalists are affected by conditions of national crisis and emergency and by colonial contexts. Most important, however, by virtue of their family and social status, loyalists are in positions of proximity or actual access to power and authority; they occupy prestigious stations in their societies.

It is apparent that loyalists and revolutionaries are similar in some ways and different in other aspects. We shall return to this topic in Chapter 6.

Symbolic Leaders

Klapp (1948, 1964) devoted much time and energy to the study of symbolic leaders and their making and unmaking. A leader or a hero, Klapp maintained, is more than just a person. He or she is an ideal, an image, and a symbol.

Symbolic leaders arise in four ways: (1) by spontaneous popular recognition and homage—as in entertainment, sports, political crises, and military conflicts; (2) by formal recognition, as in presidential elections and military decorations; (3) by the gradual growth of popular legends; and (4) by the poetic creations of dramatists, novelists, and writers.

Klapp identifies six types of symbolic leaders: (1) the conquering hero, who demonstrates superhuman powers and performs invincible feats—for example, Siegfried; (2) the Cinderella, who as the underdog somehow prevails through a miraculous deed—for instance, David of David and Goliath fame; (3) the clever hero, who prevails by dint of his or her wit and brain—for example, Robin Hood; (4) the delivering and avenging hero, who enters in a dramatic moment to save people from danger or distress—for instance, Moses; (5) the benefactor, who aids the poor and the unfortunate—for example, Babe Ruth (who presented sick boys with bats); and (6) the martyr, who suffers and sacrifices for the public good—for instance, Gandhi.[1]

The functions of symbolic leaders are to excite popular interest and imagination, to distinguish heroes from villains, to convey a social message, and to respond to human need for community.

The unmaking of symbolic leaders takes place through defeat, weakness, or cowardice; or through loss of glamour, support, or status.

Brown (1960) studied American presidential campaign biographies as attempts to create symbolic leaders through propaganda. Focusing on the period 1824–1960, he concluded that the function of the campaign biography is to present the candidate as "*the* ideal citizen of the Republic." More specific, the candidate is a man of northern European ancestry; his parents are admirable folk, who have reared their son in "patriotic virtue and Christian piety"; he grows up in humble circumstances, enjoying a happy, active boyhood; through education and hard work, he rises above the station in life into which he was born; he serves with distinction in the armed forces and "covers himself with glory"; his occupations have included farming, law, business, or politics; he has a record of civic and community service; he is "surrounded by a dutiful, loving wife and adoring children"; he is a man of "impeccable moral character and of sturdy republican virtues"; he is "an enduring symbol of the ideals and aspirations of the Republic" (Brown 1960, 144–45; emphasis in original).

Manufactured Leaders

Kennan and Hadley (1986) are political consultants who have had experience with mayoral, gubernatorial, senatorial, and presidential candidates—both incumbents and challengers). Their "creation of a political leader operational flow" is based on the assumption that a political candidate is a consumer product much like cottage cheese or toothpaste. The "operational flow" has two components:

A.   The candidate's political campaign group:

1. The creators: (a) the media consultants; (b) the campaign manager; (c) the creative researcher, who sets direction; (d) the evaluative researcher, who tests currents.

2. The implementers: (a) producers of TV advertising, (b) producers of print advertising, (c) the field force of volunteers and workers, (d) the surrogates who organize meetings and make speeches on behalf of the candidate.

3. The candidate as a puppet whose strings are being pulled by the creators and the implementers.

B.   The campaign phases: voters and their perceptions:

1. 9–18 months before the election: understanding the voters and their perceptions.

2. 7–14 months before the election: identification and accentuation of issues.

3. 4–8 months before the election: shaping and introducing the candidate.

4. Throughout the campaign: reassessment and fine tuning.

Kennan and Hadley reflect on the "operational flow" by raising and responding to two questions: (1) Why is this process so successful? Because of the increasing importance of the media as definers and interpreters of reality, and because of the increasing importance of those who can manipulate the media. (2) Are the people who are elected by this process political leaders? No, if a leader is one who has a vision and motivates others. Yes, if a leader is a political manager who reflects what people want to see and hear.

MILITARY LEADERS

Replicating their studies of revolutionaries and loyalists discussed above, Rejai and Phillips (1996) focused on forty-five famous military leaders from thirteen countries spread over four continents and four centuries. Once again, they deployed an interactional theory, stressing the interplay between sociodemographic variables, psychological dynamics, and situational forces. They gathered uniform data on the military leaders with the aim of answering two questions: What are their sociodemographic backgrounds? What propels them toward the military profession?

As for sociodemographic variables, Rejai and Phillips found that military leaders are mature men (over 45) upon reaching the highest rank, though they are exposed to military ideology—and participate in combat—early in life, sometimes in their teens. Although a majority of military leaders are rural-born, *all* military elites develop early and sustained exposure to urban cultures. Military leaders come from the main ethnic and religious groupings of their societies. They are well educated, with an overwhelming majority graduating from military academies.

Military leaders are overwhelmingly committed to the military as their sole occupation, although in retirement some follow a variety of other pursuits. The primary occupations of the fathers of military leaders are primarily the military and the professions, with a smattering of other pursuits. Military leaders adopt conservative and indigenous political ideologies; radical or foreign ideologies are extremely rare. Military leaders have a dualistic view of human nature, distinguishing between good (their own people) and evil (other peoples). Military leaders have a uniformly positive view of their own countries, while their attitude toward the international community is dualistic, distinguishing friends and enemies.

The socioeconomic status of military leaders has undergone significant changes in recent times. To be more precise, in the twentieth century upper class representation has significantly dropped, while middle and lower class representation has risen sharply. In other words, increasingly the military has become an avenue of upward social mobility.

As for psychological variables, Rejai and Phillips identified six dynamics. To one degree or another, all military leaders are, almost by definition, *nationalists*: they are intensely committed to their countries and they seek to enhance the prestige and power of their nations. Over one-third of military leaders exhibit some form of *imperialist* design: they seek to improve the status of their nations at the expense of other countries. Nearly half of military leaders experience *relative deprivation*, defined as perception of discrepancy between aspiration and achievement. Nearly 40 percent of military leaders experience *love deprivation*, defined as the loss of one or both parents in childhood, the bereavement resulting in an attempt to compensate by substituting the military for the homes they lost. More than one-third of military leaders experience social, cultural, physical, medical, or psychological *marginality*: they deviate in perceptible ways from standard norms. Nearly half of the military leaders are given to *vanity and egotism*, some as means of compensating for their marginality. On the whole, the most pervasive psychological dynamic is nationalism, followed by vanity, relative deprivation, love deprivation, imperialism, and marginality.

As for situational considerations, four variables emerged. *Birthplace*: Twenty percent of military leaders are born in garrison towns or similar circumstances that are conducive to military careers. *Family influences*: Nearly two-thirds of military leaders are either born directly to military families or are influenced to choose a military career by a family member or a close family friend. *National crises*: Over 20 percent of military leaders steer toward the military in response to situations of national crisis or emergency. *Luck or chance*: A few individuals join the military because of fortuitous or unanticipated circumstances. Clearly, the most compelling situational dynamics are family influences, followed distantly by national crisis and birthplace, and very remotely by luck or chance.

SUMMARY

In this chapter we have discussed seven types of leaders under three broad headings: (1) transforming leaders: charismatic, revolutionary, and entrepreneurial; 2) transactional leaders: loyalist, symbolic, and manufactured; and (3) military leaders. Some of these types are more fully elaborated than others, but we have said enough about each type to convey substantive understanding. Undoubtedly, we have not exhausted the topic, but we have developed a reasonable grasp of the principal kinds of leaders we are likely to encounter in human societies.

NOTE

1. Klapp (1964) revised this sixfold typology as follows: (1) the hero, (2) the incorruptible, (3) the object of desire, (4) the popular villain, (5) the comic figure, and (6) the popular victim.

CHAPTER 4

Motivations of Leaders

What motivates a person to become a leader? This deceptively simple question continues to elude theorists and researchers in the social and behavioral sciences. Although we have addressed this issue at several junctures in Chapter 3, it is now time to undertake a more systematic and comprehensive treatment.

A perusal of the extant literature reveals four broad approaches to the study of motivation: the psychoanalytic, the psychohistorical, the empirical, and the experimental. These approaches deal with a variety of leaders: social, political, revolutionary, religious, and the like. The psychoanalytic approach focuses on the inner dynamics of human personality, and it seeks to locate the impulse to leadership activity in the psychology of individuals. The psychohistorical approach seeks to move beyond pure psychoanalysis by placing personality dynamics in the context of society and history; it attempts to combine psychological motivation with actual life experiences as an individual moves through time. The empirical approach focuses on scientific investigation of experiences of actual leaders in sociopolitical contexts. The experimental approach introduces a whole new dimension by studying neurochemical properties of individual leaders. We shall consider each approach in turn.

THE PSYCHOANALYTIC APPROACH

The Leader as Primal Father and Ego Ideal

Pioneered by Sigmund Freud, the psychoanalytic approach constitutes the foundation of some influential studies of leadership. *Group Psychology and the Analysis of the Ego* (Freud [1921] 1960) presents a theory of leadership in general. More explicit applications of the Freudian theory to political and revolutionary personalities have been undertaken by Lasswell ([1930] 1960, 1948) and Wolfenstein (1967), among others.

The psychology of the leader, according to Freud, stands in sharp contrast to that of the followers (see Chapter 2). Most specific, the leader has no emotional ties to anyone; he is "absolutely narcissistic." To quote Freud:

[F]rom the first there were two kinds of psychologies, that of the individual members of the group and that of the father, chief, or leader. The members of the group were subject to ties just as we see them today, but the father of the primal horde was free. His intellectual acts were strong and independent even in isolation, and his will needed no reinforcement from others. Consistency leads us to assume that his ego had few libidinal ties; he loved no one but himself, or other people only in so far as they served his needs. . . .

He, at the very beginning of the history of mankind, was the "superman" whom Nietzsche only expected from the future. Even today the members of a group stand in need of the illusion that they are equally and

justly loved by their leader; but the leader himself
need love no one else, he may be of a masterful
nature, absolutely narcissistic, self-confident and
independent. (Freud [1921] 1960, 71)

Freud's conception of leadership is based upon his
controversial theory of "primal horde," borrowed from
Charles Darwin (Freud [1921] 1960, 69). According to this
theory, at the dawn of human society a primal horde of
rebellious sons killed their tyrannical father and founded
a fraternal society. The need for leadership soon reasserted
itself, however, finding expression in totemism and
religion, the totem and the deity being the reincarnations
of the murdered father. Writes Freud:

The leader of the group is still the dreaded primal
father; the group still wishes to be governed by
unrestricted force; it has an extreme passion for
authority; in Le Bon's phrase, it has a thirst for
obedience. The primal father is the group ideal, which
governs the ego in place of the ego ideal. (Freud
[1921] 1960, 76)

The Displacement Hypothesis

Acknowledging the "spectacular and influential nature of
Freud's work," Lasswell ([1930] 1960, 17), focuses
directly upon the psychological dynamics of political
leaders. Relying also on Adler's ([1928] 1966) concept of
"will to power," he views the political personality as the
power-centered personality: the political leader compen-
sates for his feelings of inadequacy and low self-esteem by
a relentless pursuit of power. He values power above all
else, since only through the pursuit and exercise of power
can he maintain his personal integrity. Moreover, this

private need/motive is displaced upon public objects and rationalized in terms of the public interest. Lasswell writes:

> The political type is characterized by an intense and ungratified craving for deference.
> These cravings, both accentuated and unsatisfied in the primary [family] circle, are displaced upon public objects. . . .
> The displacement is rationalized in terms of the public interest. (Lasswell 1948, 38; Lasswell [1930] 1960, passim; cf. George 1969)

Lasswell's ground-breaking work on a wide range of clinical case studies led him to postulate several types of political personalities, most notably the agitator, the administrator, and the theorist/ideologue. The agitator is committed to principle, highly narcissistic (cf. Freud), and dependent on the emotional acclamation of the people. Lasswell writes:

> The hallmark of the agitator is the high value which he places on the response of the public. As a class the agitators are strongly narcissistic types. Narcissism is encouraged by obstacles encountered in the early love relationships, or by overindulgence and admiration in the family circle. Libido is blocked in moving outward toward objects and settles back upon the self. Sexual objects which are like the self are preferred, and a strong homoerotic component is thus characteristic. Among the agitators yearning for emotional response of the homoerotic kind is displaced upon generalized objects, and high value is put on arousing emotional responses from the community at large. (Lasswell [1930] 1960, 262)

The administrators, by contrast, displace their private motives upon impersonal and concrete objects:

As a group the administrators are distinguished by the value which they place upon the coordination of effort in continuing activity. They differ from the agitators in that their affects are displaced on less remote and abstract objects. . . . They display an impersonal interest in the task of organization itself, and assert themselves with firmness . . . in professional and intimate life. . . . Tied neither to abstractions nor to particular people, they are able to deal with both in a context of human relations, impersonally conceived. (Lasswell [1930] 1960, 263–64)

The ideologue is ridden by doubt, preoccupied with trivialities, committed to "truth," and dogmatic:

Dogma is a defensive reaction against doubt in the mind of the theorist [i.e., the ideologue], but of doubt of which he is unaware. The unconscious hatred of authority [which entails "a measure of self-punishment"] discloses itself in the endless capacity of the theorist to imagine new reasons for disbelief, and in his capacity to labor over trivialities, and to reduce his whole intellectual scheme to a logical absurdity. . . . Deep doubts about the self are displaced on to doubts about the world outside, and these doubts are sought to be allayed by ostentatious preoccupation with truth. (Lasswell [1930] 1960, 175)

Lasswell sees all political leaders in the same light: the displacement of private motives upon public objects. Anticipating the work of Wolfenstein, he writes: "The effects which are organized in the family are redistributed upon various social objects, such as the state. Political crises are complicated by the concurrent reactivation of specific primitive impulses" (Lasswell [1930] 1960, 264).

Oedipal Conflict Writ Large

Wolfenstein's (1967) study of "the revolutionary personality" is in essence a specific application and amplification of Lasswell's displacement hypothesis, focusing on the Oedipal complex. Whereas in Freud the rebellious sons channeled their aggression directly against the father, in Wolfenstein they externalize their aggression onto larger arenas.

Wolfenstein employs Erik H. Erikson's epigenetic model (see the psychohistorical approach below) of the eight stages of personality development—oral, anal, genital, latency, adolescence, young manhood, adulthood, and maturity—in an effort to locate the motivational dynamics that impel men toward revolutionary action. He searches for similarities and differences in the early life experiences of Lenin, Trotsky, and Gandhi in an attempt to account for their emergence as revolutionary personalities in later years.

Wolfenstein's exclusive concern, we should note, is with the psychological dimension of Erikson's formulation, leaving out altogether social, historical, and cultural variables: "My interest has been quite exclusively in the motivations of the subjects and certain emotional capabilities related to these" (Wolfenstein 1967, 302).

According to Erikson, as we shall see, each stage of personality development is marked by a distinctive crisis (or set of crises), the successful resolution of which is a prerequisite for a "mature" transition to the succeeding stage. Focusing on the genital stage, Wolfenstein identifies the inability to manage its unique crisis—the Oedipal complex—as the root motivation of the revolutionary. This uniformity, he finds, contrasts sharply with the life experiences of Lenin, Trotsky, and Gandhi in the other stages of personality development.

Wolfenstein concludes that the revolutionary personality represents the externalization of the parental conflict associated with the Oedipal complex and its projection at the societal level: "the revolutionist is the one who escapes from the burdens of Oedipal guilt and ambivalence by carrying his conflict with authority into the political realm." He adds:

> The basic attribute of this personality is that it is based on opposition to governmental authority; this is the result of the individual's continuing need to express his aggressive impulses vis-à-vis his father and the repressive action of governmental officials. The latter permits the individual to externalize his feelings of hatred. . . . Now the situation is much less ambivalent; governmental authority is clearly malevolent . . . and hence can be fought with a clear conscience. And because . . . the aggressive governmental action came as a consequence of individual actions which were representative [of the way in which government treats the "people"], rather than personal, the individual finds a cause to defend. . . . [At first] the cause is crudely conceived and unelaborated; with time an ideological superstructure is based upon it so that the individual can fulfill his needs for self-justification.
>
> In this manner the revolutionist dichotomizes his world, and with it the emotional complex of his ambivalent feelings toward his father. As a consequence his feelings of guilt are substantially reduced, so that in all three cases we saw the men turning from introspection and inaction to vigorous pursuance of

their revolutionary vocations. (Wolfenstein 1967, 308–309)

Governmental authority, then, is the functional equivalent of a surrogate father. Each of the three revolutionaries, Wolfenstein notes, fashioned an ideological framework which, among other things, juxtaposed the functional equivalent of a benevolent father (communist society, national independence) to that of a malevolent one (czarism, British imperialism). The resolution of the guilt and ambivalence permits all hatred to be directed toward the government, all love toward the "people."

Phaeton Complex and Political Leadership

Lucille Iremonger (1970) studied twenty-four successive British prime ministers, from Spencer Perceval in 1809 to Neville Chamberlain who resigned in 1940. She found that fifteen of the twenty-four men (62.5 percent) had lost one or both parents before reaching age fifteen. She considered this figure exceptionally high, the risk of bereavement for the general population was then 10–15 percent.

For theoretical insight, Iremonger turned to the French psychoanalyst Maryse Choisy, whose study of bastards had led her to theorize that the child who is deprived of love in the family quests after power and acclaim in the political arena. Moreover, Choisy discovered, bastards develop a harsh and rigid superego, are very narcissistic, and are driven to fantasies of omnipotence. Furthermore, Choisy found, bastards are characterized by abnormal sensitivity, chronic depression, and a belief in magic. Finally, Choisy maintained, given the absence of a father figure, bastards hark back to the myth of Phaeton, not Oedipus.[1]

Iremonger theorized that losing one or both parents in childhood produces most of the same consequences of bastardy. She wrote:

> The deeper I plunged into the lives of my chosen two dozen, the more strongly did a pattern emerge. Not only had many of these men suffered the traumatic and unusual experience of lack of love in their early years. So many were abnormally sensitive, reserved, and isolated. So many demonstrated the most powerful drives for attention and affection. So many . . . had benefited in childhood from the devotion and inspired teaching . . . of outstanding and immensely self-confident mentors. . . . So many of them . . . in maturity, had drunk deep from the self-forgetting, totally loving, support of adoring women. In so many, too, the need for, and dependence on, such . . . love was blatant, even compulsive. Perhaps more significant still, their hunger for it when it was denied them, and their desperate search to find it, was often almost pitiable. (1970, 11; cf. 308–309)

In general, Iremonger found her subjects to have developed grandiose self-concepts; to have suffered from crippling physical, medical, or psychological handicaps; to have been hypersensitive in nature and to have experienced psychosomatic disorders; to have been solitary and unhappy figures; to have led austere and ascetic lives; to have been depressive personalities; to have been shy and timid; to have been superstitious and given to mysticism; to have had a compulsive and obsessive need for love throughout their lives; and to have exhibited periodic recklessness of a suicidal nature.

THE PSYCHOHISTORICAL APPROACH

While the psychoanalytic perspective deals predominantly with the inner dynamics of human personality, the psychohistorical approach attempts to move beyond psychoanalysis by placing personality dynamics in the context of society and history. As pioneered by Erik H. Erikson ([1942] 1963, 1962, 1969) and practiced by many others, the psychohistorical approach represents, by definition, a fusion of psychology and history. In particular, in Erikson's interpretation, it seeks to juxtapose and interrelate the personality conflicts of a "great man" with the historical problems of a particular era.

The Crises of Personality Development

According to Erikson's "epigenetic principle," the human life cycle consists of eight distinct and successive stages, each of which involves a sociohistorical setting and each of which contributes the progressive differentiation—and wholeness—of the human personality as it unfolds through time. Each stage is characterized by a distinct crisis or turning point, the successful addressing of which contributes the development of a fully psychosocial personality. These crises represent life tasks as the individual adjusts (or fails to adjust) to his historical setting and to the accompanying demands of sociopolitical institutions. As such, the crises have both negative and positive potential: they may function as sources of weakness as well as of strength. They may generate innovation and creativity or, alternatively, stagnation and despair.

According to Erikson's "epigenetic chart"—a modification and elaboration of Freud's stage theory—there are eight phases of human development. The first stage is the oral-sensory, and its characteristic crisis concerns the child's development of a sense of trust or mistrust depending on the extent to which his[2] needs for love, comfort, and security are met. The crisis of the second stage, the muscular-anal, is that of autonomy versus shame and doubt. The successful resolution of this conflict results in the development of a sense of pride, autonomy, and self-esteem; failure brings feelings of shame, doubt, and inadequacy.

The turning point of the third stage, the locomotor-genital, is the Oedipal complex. Here the child must resolve the problem of guilt growing out of ambivalent feelings toward his parents. The fourth stage—and the last period of childhood—is latency, and its crisis is that of industry versus inferiority. Here the child must expand his horizons, develop proficiency in dealing with new peoples and situations, and overcome the feelings of hostility—as well as subordination—to his father.

The fifth stage is adolescence, and its turning point is the most prominent concept with which Erikson has been associated: identity crisis. According to Erikson, identity represents a cumulative accretion of self-confidence. Its opposite—identity diffusion or identity confusion—occurs between the ages of sixteen and twenty-four. In the interim between childhood and young manhood, each youth must construct for himself a perspective on his past and an outlook for his future—a sense of integrity, a sense of direction, a sense of continuity.

The search for identity may involve a "moratorium," a period of time in which one is neither a carefree child nor a fully responsible adult but something in between. This postponement allows the individual to test and to experiment, without being held strictly responsible for his every action. The moratorium allows the individual to grow toward a psychosocial whole.

The search for identity typically entails a turn to ideologies or thought systems—at times totalistic—that enhance the individual's personal integrity and social solidarity. Ideologies, whether political or religious, counteract identity diffusion and put the individual at one with the social whole. As such, Erikson notes, identity and ideology are two sides of the same coin.

The sixth stage of personality development is young manhood, and its turning point is the conflict between intimacy and isolation. Here the individual must determine the nature of his relationship to his peers, especially of the opposite sex. The maintenance of one's individuality must be balanced against the need for intimacy on the one hand and the threat of isolation on the other.

The crisis of the seventh stage, adulthood, is that of generativity versus stagnation. Once the identity and intimacy crises have been overcome, the individual faces the problem of generativity—that is, of establishing and guiding the next generation. This crisis may be confronted either in terms of actual parenthood or symbolically in terms of accomplishments or "works." The last stage is that of maturity, and its crisis is that of ego integration versus despair. Either an individual maintains spiritual integrity and continues to contribute to the social whole, or he falls into a state of despair in the face of advancing years.

Personal Crisis and Historical Trauma

Erikson's theory of the life cycle and his psychohistorical perspective were presented for the first time in *Childhood and Society* (1963), first published in 1950. Subsequently they were systematically applied in his two ground-breaking studies of Martin Luther and Mahatma Gandhi (Erikson 1962, 1969). Erikson's initial concern with problems of childhood grew to incorporate the crisis of adolescence (Luther) and the turning point of adulthood (Gandhi). His interest in great historic figures was, in turn, sparked by a 1942 study of Adolf Hitler, in which Erikson seeks to relate personality dynamics and historic transformation.

Predictably, Erikson analyzes Hitler along two dimensions: his personal and psychological needs and drives, and the sociohistorical setting of Weimar Germany. As for the first, he notes Hitler's persistent struggle against difficult odds, the traumas generated by "a drunkard and a tyrant" father, the "pathological attachment to his mother," the "horror of Jewry," the moodiness, stubbornness, rebelliousness, and so on (Erikson [1942] 1963, 329, 338, 342). On the other hand, Erikson stresses the many crises of the Weimar Republic, the lingering and bitter memories of defeat in the first war, the disintegration of social and cultural institutions, and Germany's lack of a solid national identity. These conditions, Erikson believes, made the Germans highly vulnerable to the appeals of Hitler for unity, solidarity, and power and to "his fanatical cries of 'Germany, Germany, Germany'" ([942] 1963, 340). It was this coincidence of personal crisis and social trauma, Erikson argues, that catapulted Hitler to prominence.

Erikson's treatments of Luther and Gandhi (Erikson 1962, 1969) are far more elaborate. In the case of Luther, the central focus is identity crisis; in the matter of Gandhi, generativity crisis. In neither case does Erikson ignore the Oedipal problems. In each case he uses a pivotal "Event" around which to organize the study.

Erikson's work on Luther opens with the account of the "Event," a fit Luther is supposed to have had in the choir of his monastery in his early twenties. Falling to the ground, according to eyewitnesses, Luther raved: "It isn't me!" (German version) or "I am *not*!" (Latin version).

Erikson treats this incident as the exemplar of Luther's identity crisis, and he searches for its dynamics in Luther's home life and childhood.

Luther's parents were strict disciplinarians, as were the teachers under whom he studied. Young Martin himself was brooding and aloof, lacked feelings, was rebellious and given to violent moods, and demonstrated a bad temper and an intense capacity to hate. At the University of Erfurt he studied under radical theologians who questioned the strict teachings of the Catholic Church. Having obtained a master's degree, he underwent an abrupt "conversion": in an act of outright rebellion against his father, Luther terminated his academic studies and decided to become a monk. Having joined a harsh and austere monastery, he was ordained a priest in 1507, at age twenty-three.

Luther's training for the priesthood—itself a form of ideological indoctrination—provided a moratorium wherein he formulated his distinctive theology as a legitimate weapon with which to attack the Catholic Church. In 1517 Luther nailed his ninety-five theses to the church door in Wittenberg.

Luther's reformulation of Christianity, his emphasis on the priesthood of all believers, his attack on Church hierarchy—in all this, according to Erikson, he spoke for countless thousands who had shared the same sentiments but who had not dared to challenge the established order. He was outraged where others were tolerant. He was outspoken where others remained silent. In short, Luther was one of those great men "called upon . . . to lift his individual patienthood to the level of a universal one and to try to solve for all what he could not solve for himself alone" (Erikson 1962, 67).

The "Event" around which Erikson constructs his study of Gandhi is the Ahmedabad textile strike of 1918.

Although other authorities—Gandhi himself included—have not assigned such signal importance to the strike, Erikson sees it not only as the cornerstone of labor unionism in India, but also as critical in Gandhi's life and in the fate of nonviolence as a transformative technique. The strike, he notes, occasioned the first time Gandhi, then forty-eight, fasted for a political cause. A year later, he led the mass movement of civil disobedience, thereby establishing a spiritual belief in nonviolence as a ritual.

In expounding and practicing nonviolence, according to Erikson, Gandhi was responding to a crisis of generativity characteristic of his adulthood. (Gandhi's relationships with his four sons were always strained.) In fashioning a following, a vast retinue, an extended family, and a nonviolent technique, Gandhi was involved in a process of nationbuilding as well of self-creation. In transforming the negative Indian identity of weakness and inferiority vis-à-vis the British, he at the same time transformed a negative self-image based on persistent feelings of depression, personal despair and humiliation, and an intense feeling of guilt toward the father (note the famous episode of Gandhi having sexual intercourse with his wife in their bedroom as his father lay on his deathbed in another room in the same house). In Gandhi's case, Erikson maintains the moratorium involved in a search for identity was provided by two decades of sojourn in England and South Africa. In any event, we witness once again the coalescence of personal needs and historical imperatives.

To summarize, each of Erikson's three figures was a great political, ideological, or religious innovator. Each was driven by powerful childhood experiences. And each stepped out of conventional boundaries to adapt the historical setting to his special needs and demands.

THE EMPIRICAL APPROACH

Departing from psychoanalysis and psychohistory, the empirical approach focuses on the actual motivational experiences of leaders across time and space.

In a study of 180 United States senators who took office between 1945 and 1957, Matthews (1960) identified four motivational factors for becoming a politician: (1) the desire for prestige and power; (2) the love of the game, the excitement, the camaraderie, the sense of being an insider; (3) the tradition of public service; and (4) the family influence and socialization coming quite early in life.

Barber (1965) conducted a study of nearly 200 Connecticut state legislators through interviews, the administration of questionnaires, and reliance on the printed media. He treated political leadership in terms of three interrelated variables: (1) Motivation: "Do I want it?" (2) Resources: "Can I do it?" (3) Opportunity: "Do they want me?"

Barber used two variables to arrive at a fourfold typology of state legislators: *activity* in the legislature and *willingness* to return. High activity and high willingness produced *Lawmaker*s. High activity and low willingness yielded *Advertisers*. Low activity and high willingness resulted in *Spectators*. Low activity and low willingness formed *Reluctants*.

Addressing the issue of motivation, Barber found that of the four types of legislators only the Lawmaker has high self-esteem, characterized by consistency between his ideal self and his perceived self. The explanation, Barber maintained, lies in the fact that for the Lawmaker politics is a primary occupation from which he derives genuine satisfaction, whereas for the other three types politics is a second choice.

Other characteristics of the Lawmaker include persistence in organizational work, seeing things through, demonstrating personal-emotional interest in politics, being secure and easygoing, having a sense of humor, and finding political life challenging and exciting.

Payne and his associates (1984) offered a more wide-ranging comparative study of why politicians enter politics. They interviewed state legislators, city councilpersons, and politicians from Australia, Colombia, France, and Venezuela; and they relied on biographies and autobiographies.

Payne and associates maintained that politicians are moved by a series of "incentives" that act as motivational guides and fulfill emotional and psychological needs. The incentives are:

1. Status: the need for prestige and public recognition.

2. Program: the need to work on concrete policy issues.

3. Conviviality: the need to please others and to gain approval.

4. Obligation: the need to follow one's conscience, engage in morally correct behavior, and expose immoral practices.

5. Game: the need to compete with others in structured and intellectually challenging interactions and to develop and implement strategies of winning.

6. Mission: the need to be so committed to a transcendent cause as to give meaning and purpose to life.

7. Adulation: the need for exaggerated praise and affection, for expression of public love and gratitude.

Payne and his colleagues concluded that the first five types of incentives are conducive to political stability, whereas the last two types foster instability.

THE EXPERIMENTAL APPROACH

In two experimental studies Madsen (1985, 1986) introduces a major twist and renders the issue of motivation virtually irrelevant. Madsen's declared objective is to give Lasswell's political personality a neurochemical foundation. What differentiates the power seeker from the nonpower seeker, Madsen maintains, is that the former has an elevated biochemical marker, whole blood serotonin (WBS), one of several neuroregulators.

Madsen's evidence comes from two sources. First, a series of studies of vervet monkeys by a team of UCLA scientists found that "among captive male vervets there is a biochemical marker for dominance." To be specific, "serotonin levels track changes in status: dominant males who become nondominant exhibit a decline in whole blood serotonin . . . whereas nondominant animals who become dominant show the reverse" (Madsen 1985, 451).

Second, Madsen sought "a loose test in humans of the UCLA group's fascinating findings" (1985, 453) by conducting a series of experiments to examine the relationship between psychological stress and distribution of influence in small social units engaged in common problem solving. The experiments involved twelve groups, each consisting of six male undergraduate UCLA students—half of the groups in high-stress conditions, the other in low.

The experiments entailed, on the one hand, the administration of a questionnaire to collect behavioral, judgmental, and attitudinal data about the subjects. The behavioral items dealt with Type A personality characteristics—aggressiveness, hostility, competitiveness, a sense of time urgency—which, according to Madsen, typify power seekers. On the other hand, a blood sample was taken from each subject every twenty minutes throughout the problem-solving sessions. These samples were assayed by the UCLA group for a number of biochemical properties, including WBS. The results were correlated with the data obtained from the questionnaire.

Madsen found that there is indeed a positive correlation between high serotonin levels and Type A personality and, therefore, power seeking and dominance. He wrote:

> [T]here is in these research results good evidence of a tie between whole blood serotonin and a power or dominance orientation in humans. That discovery echoes similar findings in a species of subhuman primates and constitutes the first systematic evidence of a biochemical property in humans that differentiates power seekers from others. (Madsen 1985, 456)

While mindful of the fact that in the UCLA studies "a high WBS level is a marker of *successful* power seeking," Madsen proceeded to insist that "WBS marks [all] power seekers, successful or not" (1985, 455; emphasis in original).

Stressing the value of "animal models" in social science research, Madsen staked out a bold claim: "one can see in this discovery clear linkage between behavioral political science and the neurosciences, which reminds us that many of the most enduring research problems in political science have investigable biological foundations." Accordingly, Madsen's own "finding represents for political science a major new direction in the behavioral study of power" (1985, 455, 456).

SUMMARY

In this chapter we have discussed four distinct approaches to the issue of leader motivation. Although intuitively attractive, the psychoanalytic and psychohistorical studies lack scientific foundation, in addition to having a Western bias and a male bias. The empirical approach has scientific validity, but the sample sizes and the range of explanation are limited.

Original though it is, the experimental approach entails some important difficulties in addition to the ones Madsen himself acknowledges (e.g., the inadequacy of questionnaire responses for establishing motivation). Most important, how does one study leaders of the past, the present, and the future? How does one administer the questionnaire, and how does one obtain the blood samples? A methodological nightmare, indeed, Madsen's work has only heuristic value of the remotest nature. This may explain the fact that as of this writing no one has followed up on Madsen's studies, promising as they were.

NOTES

1. In Greek mythology, Phaeton, being unsure of his legitimacy, developed illusions of grandeur and supernatural powers; sought grandiose compensation in acclaim and adoration for childhood deprivation; being inexperienced, recklessly drove an uncontrollable chariot across the sky threatening the cosmic order; and was struck dead by a thunderbolt.

2. As is the case with most psychological theorists, Erikson's orientation is exclusively masculine.

CHAPTER 5

Functions of Leaders

This chapter addresses three interrelated questions: What do leaders do? What functions do they perform? Why—and how—are they important to individuals and societies?

A perusal of the literature finds the emergence of six sets of leader functions as central: moral purpose, national unity, system functions (social stability), fulfillment of human needs, fulfillment of personal needs, and certain evolutionary functions. We shall consider each in turn.

MORAL PURPOSE

As we have seen in Chapter 1, Burns (1978) identifies several characteristics of leadership. To reiterate some of the main points, leadership is collective: it responds to the mutual needs and wants of both leaders and followers. Leadership is purposeful: it leads to the creation of ideas, movements, institutions, and nations. Leadership is of two types: transactional and transforming. Transactional leadership rests on the exchange of one thing for another (e.g., jobs for votes). Transforming leadership seeks the moral elevation of both leaders and followers, which may require sacrifices all around. "True" leadership is morally uplifting, and the true leader is a moral agent.

NATIONAL UNITY

Shils and Young (1953) and Katz and Dayan (1986) maintain that leaders provide national ritual and national communion; they reaffirm national moral consensus; and they manage conflict and dissent.

Focusing on the 1953 Coronation of Queen Elizabeth II, Shils and Young hold that the Coronation provided for national unity and reinforced moral consensus. "The sacredness of a society," they write, "is at bottom the sacredness of its moral rules," and these rules require periodic reaffirmation (1953, 66). As such, "the Coronation was the ceremonial occasion for the affirmation of the moral values by which the society lives. It was an act of national communion" (1953, 67). And again: "The Coronation Service and the Procession which followed were shared and celebrated by nearly all the people of Britain. In these events . . . the Queen and her people were [through the media and the attendant festivities] . . . brought into a great nationwide communion" (1953, 70–71).

Writing on "Contests, Conquests, and Coronation: On Media Events and Their Heroes," Katz and Dayan (1986) argue that the media depend upon, create, and report on heroes and heroic roles, just as the heroes depend on the media for reportage and attention. In other words, heroic status depends on the media, and the media depend on heroes. As examples Katz and Dayan cite Henry Kissinger's shuttle diplomacy, Pope John Paul II in Poland, the Kennedy funerals, and the Olympic games. They write: "Each of these events is also a ceremony celebrating the unity of a nation or of several nations" (1986, 137). Moreover, people participate in these events as "the expression of *communitas*" (139).

More specific, *contests* are broadcasts of ceremonial competitions between individuals or nations, such as Wimbledon, the World Cup, or the Super Bowl. *Conquests* are broadcasts of "great steps for mankind," whereby a hero "facing insuperable odds, enters the enemy camp unarmed, as did . . . Sadat in Jerusalem" (Katz and Dayan 1986, 141). *Coronations* are the rights of passage of great individuals.

Contests, conquests, and coronations are also ways of managing conflict; they are "ceremonial occasions in which conflict is put into the larger perspective of the basic values of a society, so that conflict can be expressed, respoken, and overcome" (Katz and Dayan 1986, 142). Contests are symbolic transformations of conflict; conquests are processes whereby conflicts evaporate in the aura of admired heroes; and coronations are suspensions of daily conflicts in order to recall shared values.

SYSTEM FUNCTIONS

Focusing on "strategic elites" in modern societies, Keller (1963) defines these elites as "a minority of individuals designated to serve a collectivity in a socially valued way" (1963, 4). Strategic elites constitute the core group in a society that represents its unity and its potential for common action. In advanced industrial societies the core group consists of four interdependent elites, each organized in a distinct way and each performing a distinct function. These elites are responsible for the material and moral well-being of the community as a whole.

Using Parsonian social systems theory (see Parsons 1951), Keller argues that the four types of leaders perform the four main functions of the social system: goal attainment, adaptation, integration, and pattern maintenance. To be more specific, goal attainment elites are political leaders whose main concern is *social purpose*. Adaptive elites are economic, military, and diplomatic leaders whose main purpose is to develop the *means* for achieving social goals. Integrative elites are religious, philosophical, and scientific leaders whose main concern is to articulate *moral standards*. Pattern-maintenance elites are artistic, literary, and cultural leaders whose main purpose is to promote *morale and unity* in a society.

As a collectivity, strategic elites play both instrumental and symbolic roles. Their instrumental role is judged by the efficiency with which they perform their functions. Their symbolic roles are three: (1) the cognitive: providing knowledge and expertise; (2) the moral: setting standards of right and wrong; and (3) the expressive: being objects of love and hate, admiration and envy.

As distinct collectivities, strategic elites are impermanent, being subject to rotation, circulation, and transformation. "Historical and empirical evidence suggests that it is the destiny of elites to decline, whether they fail or succeed" (Keller 1963, 261).

HUMAN NEEDS

Maslow ([1950] 1970) developed a hierarchy of human needs which, he maintained, is both genetic and universal. Davies (1963, 1986) adapted Maslow's hierarchy for sociopolitical use.

According to the Maslow-Davies formulation, human needs take two forms: substantive and instrumental. Four in number, substantive needs are hierarchical and sequential: that is, each lower order of needs must be met before each higher order becomes operational (or "kicks in").

Substantive needs include: (1) physical/survival: the need for food, clothing, shelter, health; (2) social/affectional: the need for belongingness, cohesion, affection; (3) self-esteem and dignity: the need to achieve a sense of worthiness and distinctiveness; (4) self-actualization: the need for fulfillment—whether artistic, cultural, religious, or athletic.

The three instrumental needs are security, knowledge, and power. Instrumental needs are nonsequential: they exist simultaneously. And they are means to substantive ends. In other words, one must acquire security, knowledge, and power in order to fulfill any or all of the substantive needs.

Political leaders provide not only instrumental needs but also methods of using instrumental needs in order to secure substantive needs, whether individual or social. Political leaders use security, knowledge, and power in order to satisfy the physical, social, self-esteem, and self-actualization needs of their peoples.

PERSONAL NEEDS

Leaders are not always concerned exclusively with the well-being of their citizens or followers. At times leaders become cynical and self-serving; they use and abuse power for personal gain; they become capricious, corrupt, and venal; in extreme cases, they persecute, terrorize, and murder their own people

Tucker (1965) maintains that personal needs of some leaders are purely pathological and psychotic. Thus, Stalin's Great Purges and Hitler's Holocausts, far from being functional to Russian and German societies, were driven by the paranoid personalities of the two leaders.

In more general terms, McLelland (1970) speaks of "the two faces of power." Negative or personal power seeks domination and treats others as means. Positive or social power seeks to achieve common goals and treats others as ends.

EVOLUTIONARY FUNCTIONS

Crook's (1986) "The Evolution of Leadership: A Preliminary Skirmish" is an attempt to apply to human societies certain observations made about the primates. In the animal kingdom, Crook argues, leader-follower interaction is determined by the following norms: (1) leadership is attributed to those possessing information needed by others for survival; (2) leadership is inherent in the possession of knowledge, usually by older female kin; (3) leadership is attributed to individuals, usually male, who afford protection; (4) leadership is acquired by competition; (5) leadership is maintained by coercion, domination, deception, and misrepresentation; (6) leadership is attributed to specific goals, where both intra- and intersex collaboration is a prime feature of the interaction.

SUMMARY

Leaders perform identifiable functions in human societies, both for themselves and for their followers. These functions range from articulating moral purpose, promoting national unity, and providing social stability to managing conflict, fulfilling human needs, acting on personal needs, and responding to evolutionary considerations.

Not all leaders are benevolent and disinterested. At times leaders use their positions to advance self-interest and to respond to pathological personal needs. To these ends they coerce, deceive, and dominate their followers. Even terror and murder cannot be ruled out.

CHAPTER 6

Comparative Studies of Leaders

Comparative studies of leaders have taken two principal forms: cross-temporal and cross-national. Cross-temporal studies focus on groups of leaders within a given country (in our case, the United States) over time. Cross-national studies focus on groups of leaders from two or more countries either at a particular point in time or over a period of time. We shall consider each set of studies in turn.

This is a vast subject. Thus, in addition to the studies presented in Chapters 3 and 7, we can only hope to convey a flavor of the most general and the most pressing materials. The interested reader should consult the Bibliography for specific studies of British, French, German, Iranian, Irish, Jamaican, Japanese, Nigerian, Portuguese, Spanish, Syrian, Turkish, and other leaders.

CROSS-TEMPORAL STUDIES

The publication of C. Wright Mills's *The Power Elite* (1956) marked a turning point in the studies of leaders in the United States. Mills was one of the first intellectual "radicals" who felt a sense of alienation from American society, especially the institution of capitalism. He criticized his fellow intellectuals for assuming a detached posture, for being coopted and corrupted, for failing their calling to bring about societal improvement through criticism and activism. In particular, Mills was wary of academic social science for being conservative, for supporting the status quo, for being irrelevant and trivial, and for not taking a moral stand.

Mills defined elites as persons commanding the key institutional hierarchies of modern societies. In particular, he argued, three subelites—the political, the economic, and the military—come together to form the power elite or the American elite.

The power elite, Mills maintained, is characterized by considerable cohesion and unity. He saw the composite profile of members of the power elite as upper class, upper income and occupational strata, native-born of native parents, largely urban, mostly Protestant, Ivy League (or military academy) educated, born to fathers from professional and business strata.

Most particularly, Mills argued, the political, the military, and the economic elites are characterized by interlocking and intra-elite circulation. That is, members of the political elite have military and economic connections and influence; members of the military elite have political and economic connections and influence; and members of the economic elite have political and military connections and influence. In short, elite members are members of more than one elite.

While the elites are self-righteous and see themselves as inherently worthy, Mills maintained that the elites—and by extension, American society—are, in effect, characterized by structural corruption and immorality. The elites are to a large extent autonomous; they operate with an irresponsible and cynical disregard for everything except self-interest; their moral responsibility is drowned in greed, wealth, and power. In a few words, having betrayed their mission, the elites are a threat to American democracy. What is needed is an educated public to redress the issues and hold the elites accountable.

As might be expected, Mills's study generated a barrage of criticism from mainstream social scientists. Specifically, he was criticized for not being empirical and scientific, for using loose terminology, for assuming (but not demonstrating) continuity and conspiracy among elites, for assuming (but not showing) unity and homogeneity of the elites, and for overlooking the pluralism of American society and the competition among elites.

The pluralist position is most comprehensively delineated by Robert A. Dahl (1958, 1961). Dahl not only criticized Mills along the lines just mentioned, he also set out to provide an alternative to Mills. Taking an empirical, scientific approach, Dahl maintained we must study actual actors and actual decisions. He defined the elite as a controlling minority whose preferences regularly prevail. This requires three conditions: (1) that there is a well-defined elite, (2) that there is an adequate sample of elite decisions for study, and (3) that the preferences of the elite regularly prevail.

Conducting a study of political decision making in New Haven, Connecticut,[1] Dahl concluded over time that New Haven—and by extension the United States—does not have a single elite but a plurality of overlapping elites depending on the issues under consideration. That is to say, according to Dahl, elite members change depending on the policies at stake. Thus, power relations are marked by "dispersed inequalities." Moreover, far from being cohesive and autonomous, elites are functionally specific and accountable. Finally, Dahl insisted, elite positions are relatively easy to access through elective office.

Subjecting Dahl's data to comprehensive reanalysis, G. William Domhoff (1978) arrived at strikingly different findings and conclusions. Specifically, Domhoff found that in New Haven, the economic elite, the social elite, and the political elite overlap to a large extent. He wrote:

> The reality in New Haven, as elsewhere, is a distinctive upper class which includes the most important business executives, bankers, and corporate lawyers in the city. Through a study of overlapping club membership lists and interlocking boards of directors, we have been able to describe in considerable detail the New Haven upper class. (Domhoff 1978, 36)

Domhoff concluded that the situation in New Haven—and in the United States—is much closer to Mills's position than to Dahl's:

> There is, then, a ruling social class in the United States. . . . The ruling class includes about .5 to 1 percent of the population, owns about 20–25 percent of all privately held wealth, receives a highly disproportionate share of the yearly national income, controls major banks and corporations, formulates economic and political programs through a series of policy networks, and dominates—at the very least—the federal government in Washington, D.C., and the city government in New Haven, Connecticut. (Domhoff 1978, 175)

CROSS-NATIONAL STUDIES

In his global study of 1,028 world leaders (heads of government) from 138 countries in the 1945–1976 period,

Jean Blondel (1980) found: (1) a mean age of about fifty upon first assuming office, with only 15 percent attaining power before age forty; (2) the almost total absence of women—only five to be exact; (3) socioeconomic status predominantly (60 percent) middle class; (4) high level of college and university education; and (5) predominance of such occupations as law, teaching, party politics, civil service—and of the military in the third world.

The normal route to leadership, Blondel found, was through ministerial ranks, though some world leaders came to power through revolution or through military intervention.

In an even more massive work covering 20,426 cabinet ministers (who worked directly under or alongside the top leaders) throughout the world during the period 1945–1981, Blondel (1985) found: (1) ministers come to office in their forties—that is, they are five to ten years younger than the top leaders; (2) women occupy only a small fraction of ministerial posts: 238 or 1.2 percent worldwide; (3) ministers are even somewhat better educated than the top leaders. Of the about 9,000 persons whose preministerial occupations could be identified, approximately 100 were white collar workers, approximately 80 were trade unionists, some 250 had manual jobs, and a handful were farmers. The remaining leaders (approximately 8,500) came from six occupational categories: the ministry, the law, civil service, engineering, teaching, and party politics. Again, the military profession dominated in the third world, the legal profession in the rest of the globe.

Rejai and Phillips (1988) undertook a comparative analysis of two distinct elite populations: (1) a group of fifty well-known loyalist leaders who sought to operate within their sociopolitical systems, and (2) a group of fifty famous revolutionary leaders who sought to overthrow those systems. The loyalists included such figures as Chiang Kai-shek, Thomas Hutchinson (the last civilian governor of Massachusetts), and Ferdinand Marcos. The revolutionaries were represented by such men as Oliver Cromwell, Nikolai Lenin, and George Washington.

Through a series of bivariate analyses, Rejai and Phillips were surprised to discover an important cluster of traits that cuts across the loyalist-revolutionary distinction and applies to all political leaders. Political elites are typically native-born to legal marriages. They are either urban-born or, if born and raised in rural areas, they develop early and sustained exposure to urban cultures. Though having a relatively large number of siblings, they tend to be either the first-born or the last-born. They are exposed to political ideology and participate in political activity early in life, sometimes in their teens. Their ethnic and religious backgrounds are of the mainstream variety. They are highly educated, frequently at exclusive schools. They are cosmopolitan, traveling far and wide and developing a variety of foreign contacts. They write on a wide range of subjects.

In what important respects do the two groups of leaders differ? Employing discriminant analysis, Rejai and Phillips found that: if a leader remains steadfast in religious beliefs; if the leader's father is a government official or in such other occupations as the military, banking and industry, the professions, or landed gentry; if the leader is in government service; if he holds a pessimistic view of human nature but a uniformly optimistic view of his own country—under this set of circumstances, we can predict with some confidence that the leader will become a loyalist rather than a revolutionary. By contrast: if a leader abandons his religion to become an atheist; if the leader's father has an occupation not included above; if the leader is not in government service; if he has an optimistic view of human nature but a fluctuating attitude towards his own country (depending on the regime in power)—under this set of circumstances, the leader is likely to become a revolutionary rather than a loyalist. (Overall, religious orientation and father's occupation as a government official have the greatest predictive value.) In short, access to political power emerged as the key variable distinguishing the loyalists from the revolutionaries.

SUMMARY

Cross-temporal studies of leaders and power in the United States have been controversial and inconclusive, and they have entailed sweeping generalizations on all sides. The power-elite position lacks scientific rigor, to be sure. The pluralist position defends the status quo and generalizes about national politics on the basis of the study of a single university community—New Haven, Connecticut. On the whole, given what we have learned about American politics since Vietnam and Watergate, one has a tendency to gravitate toward the power-elite posture.

Cross-national studies of leaders are more dispassionate and analytical. They have gone some distance in shedding light on the traits, attributes, and characteristics of political elites.

NOTE

1. Dahl's study spans the period from 1784 (the date of New Haven's incorporation) to 1959 (closing of data collection), with particular emphasis on the 1950s.

CHAPTER 7

Women Leaders

WOMEN AND LEADERSHIP

Leadership historically has been a masculine concept and a male domain. Accordingly, virtually all theory and research have been focused on men. Women are relegated to a few traditional roles: nurses, librarians, secretaries, teachers, volunteer workers.

Beginning in the 1960s the picture started to change. As women became more active and assertive, attitudes toward them began to undergo a gradual transformation. However, even today women are not fully an integral part of theory and research, and there are only a few studies of gender differences in leadership. In practice, women hold few leadership positions and are paid lower salaries. This is true of public and private organizations, corporations and universities, cabinets and parliaments.

The principal reasons for the inferior status of women are sex role socialization and gender stereotyping. Sex role socialization means that men are brought up to be fighters and lovers and to look after the affairs of the state. By contrast, women are brought up to be wives and mothers and to look after family and children. In other words, men are socialized to be tough and macho, women to be emotional and submissive. The result was a systematic undermining of the female self-esteem.

Recent research has established that sex role socialization has been a practice invented by men in order to maintain a masculine status quo; that men and women are not all that different; that while men stress independence and autonomy, women stress interdependence and affiliation; that women are guided by the ethics of justice and fairness more than men. In short, to use the title of Carol Gilligan's famous book (1982), women speak "in a different voice."

Gender stereotyping has had equally deleterious effects on women, the general assumption being that women lack the necessary attributes, skills, attitudes, and motivations to compete in a man's world. The male stereotype portrays men as dominant, assertive, independent, competitive, risk-taking, task-oriented, and high on the need for power and achievement. The female stereotype pictures women as passive, submissive, interdependent, emotional, expressive, cooperative, person oriented, and low on the need for power and achievement.

Recent research has found that these stereotypes are without scientific foundation. The only established differences are that women rank higher than men on expressiveness and lower on advanced mathematical ability; that men are higher on task orientation and women on person orientation; that men are more confrontational and women more indirect; that assumptions of female inferiority are to be found in situational and organizational contexts, task environments, group composition, and power structure. It has also been found that gender differences are due to men's better access to social, political, and economic resources.

Thus, gender differences have been overexaggerated. Men and women are not that different; human behavior is a function of context or situation, not gender.

As these realizations became widespread, as the women's movement gained momentum, as women gained increasing self-confidence and self-esteem, and as women became increasingly active and assertive—as time passed, in short—the doors gradually opened and women found themselves involved in social, political, economic, and military roles. Occurring first in the United States and Western Europe, this phenomenon spread to become worldwide. Today women play important leadership roles at the transnational, national, and subnational (community) levels. We shall consider each in turn.

TRANSNATIONAL LEADERS

Vallance and Davies (1986) undertook a study of the women members of the European Parliament (MEPs), raising three questions: (1) Who are they? (2) Why do they seek political office? (3) Why are they better represented in the European Parliament (EP), the 500-plus-member legislative arm of the European Union, than in national legislatures of European countries?

Gathering data through interviews and the printed media on the seventy-five women MEPs in office in 1984, Vallance and Davies found: (1) the mean age for the subjects was forty-nine; (2) the subjects were married with children; (3) the subjects were well educated in law, politics, economics, languages, and the arts; (4) the subjects held professional occupations in law, journalism, academia, and business; (5) the subjects had supportive husbands. On the basis of these findings, Vallance and

Davies speculated that women MEPs are similar to female European political leaders in general.

As for the second question of why they seek office, Vallance and Davies found that the women MEPs tended to come from political families where they had been properly socialized not to be intimidated by men. Moreover, the women's professional backgrounds encouraged activism and involvement.

As for the third question of greater representation in the European Parliament, Vallance and Davies stressed the relative newness of the EP and the fluidity of the roles therein, the progressive and nonconfrontational nature of the EP, the fact that campaigning for EP is not exceedingly rigorous, and the fact that the EP is largely a discussion forum, rather than a decision-making body. For these and related reasons, some European men do not take a serious interest in the European Parliament.

Finally, Vallance and Davies found that the women in the EP tended to lean toward the center and the left, that they are more diligent and hard-working than men, and that they do not adopt a uniform posture toward women's issues.

NATIONAL LEADERS

The United States being a stronghold of feminist activism, in recent times women have scored many political victories at the congressional, gubernatorial, mayoral, and other levels. Geraldine Ferraro, the unsuccessful Democratic vice-presidential candidate in the 1984 presidential election, reached the highest political pinnacle ever occupied by an American woman. The emergence in 1997 of Madeleine Albright as Secretary of State marked a major step forward for the feminist movement.

Setting aside the United States for the time being, in this section we focus on twelve women who have risen to positions of national leadership worldwide, either as presidents or prime ministers (cf. Genovese 1993). The twelve women are: Corazon Aquino of the Philippines, Benazir Bhutto of Pakistan, Gro Harlem Brundtland of Norway, Kim Campbell of Canada, Edith Crésson of France, Violeta Chamorro of Nicaragua, Tansu Çiller of Turkey, Indira Gandhi of India, Golda Meir of Israel, Isabel Perón of Argentina, Hanna Suchocka of Poland, and Margaret Thatcher of Great Britain.

It is by now a truism that the most significant difference between men who rise to positions of national leadership and those who choose to mount revolutionary upheavals is purely and simply access to political power. Such diverse revolutionary figures as George Washington and Fidel Castro have visions of a better and more just world that they can achieve only through political power. Thwarted in their quest for access to those positions of power, they rely on violence as a way of contesting the established system. Washington, unsuccessful in his bid to expand his landholdings, came into direct conflict with English law. He was also personally affected by the Stamp and Navigation acts. Failing to reform the system to the advantage of himself and others in his situation, he embraced the radicalism that led to the American revolution. Similarly, were it not for the Batista coup of March 1952, which suspended the Cuban constitution and political processes, Castro, who at the time was campaigning for a parliamentary seat in the upcoming June elections, might have turned out to be a regular politician.

To take a more contemporary case, George Bush, by contrast, had access to political power from early in his career. Appointed to high office by several presidents, Bush was elected vice-president of the United States in

1980. His successful presidential candidacy in 1988 simply and unequivocally documents the role of access in political ascendancy.

Women have been thwarted by the long-standing tradition that favors male political leadership, by socialization patterns that negate the cultivation of traits and attributes that prepare them for leadership roles, and by life patterns that do not place them into positions of potential access to political power. Despite these setbacks, some women do achieve legitimate leadership positions. Elected women political leaders such as Aquino, Bhutto, and Gandhi achieve positions of national prominence in a political world almost totally dominated by men. What allows such women to come to power? How do they overcome tradition and gender socialization patterns? How do they reach national political leadership? A review of the paths to power for contemporary women is in order.

Some women such as Margaret Thatcher of Great Britain, Kim Campbell of Canada, Edith Crésson of France, Gro Harlem Brundtland of Norway, and Hanna Suchocka of Poland are elected to political office in ways that follow paths of access to power typically associated with men. Each of these women, mostly from the more industrialized nations of the world, appears to be selected through a path of coalition building and electoral politics, without the advantage of family position or favor. These few women function in societies that, more than most in the world, have had paths to political leadership open to women for some time. These opportunities for women are, to use an old phrase, few and far between. Most women cannot expect to rise to positions of national prominence; the chances are infinitesimally small. Yet, in some cases, one finds upon investigation that these women have experienced nontraditional political socialization. For example, while most media speak of Margaret Thatcher's

father as a grocer, further exploration shows that Alfred
Roberts was politically active all through his adult life,
rising from school governor to the position of mayor of his
city, Grantham. Thatcher's father encouraged her to move
into political activity early in life. She responded by
marrying a wealthy man whose resources released her
from the usual household and maternal duties. Without the
burden of child care and housework, Margaret Thatcher
was free to pursue a public career.

Other women who hold positions of national leadership,
particularly in modernizing countries, have risen to power
as a result of the mantle or cloak of family prominence
passing to them from father or husband. Usually the only
surviving family member of a dead or martyred political
leader, the woman who is the appropriate age or possesses
the minimal requisite skills for leadership cultivates the
followers associated with her dead family member to
maintain and perpetuate his power.

Corazon Aquino was elected president of the Philippines
following the assassination of her husband, Benigno
Aquino. A leader of the opposition to Ferdinand Marcos,
autocratic leader of the Philippines for two decades,
Benigno Aquino had remained outside the Philippines for
years prior to his death. After the assassination, his
followers and others appealed to Corazon Aquino to
challenge Marcos in the upcoming election. A quiet and
traditional woman, Corazon Aquino would never have
been interested personally in high political office, but
accepted the political role to perpetuate the beliefs, ideals,
and following of her dead husband. Supported by the
United States, her candidacy was successful.

Similarly, Benazir Bhutto of Pakistan accepted the
mantle of leadership from her martyred father, Zulfikar Ali
Bhutto, former prime minister of Pakistan, to challenge the
power of General Mohammed Zia ul-Haq, who had ruled

under martial law for eleven years. When pursuing a political career as a single woman became a liability, Benazir Bhutto accepted an arranged marriage with Asif Zardari. (Even women politicians at the national level must maintain their legitimacy within their societies.) Campaigning on the appeal of her martyred father's memory, Benazir Bhutto became the first woman to head a contemporary Muslim state and the youngest head of a fledgling democracy.

By her own account, Violeta Chamorro, widow of Pedro Joaquín Chamorro, slain owner of the newspaper *La Prensa* and one of the most active opposition figures in Nicaragua until his assassination in 1978, considered her life's work to be that of taking care of her husband, children, and home. Encouraged to take up candidacy for the presidency, Violeta Chamorro coalesced sufficient local support and American support as a result of her husband's martyrdom to be elected president in February of 1990. A measure of her socialization to roles unaccustomed to the exercise of political power at the national level is the widely reputed belief that her son-in-law, Antonio Lacayo, is the real power behind the throne.

One of the most famous women political leaders of the late twentieth century, Indira Gandhi of India, was carefully trained by her father, Jawaharlal Nehru, India's first prime minister. Many of his hopes for the political future of India were placed upon his daughter, his only child, although he asserted publicly that he wanted no role in choosing his successor. After the sudden death of Prime Minister Shastri in 1966, the Congress Party President Kamaraj chose Indira Gandhi for succession. Her ascendancy to the position of prime minister was not without an open contest, but the overwhelming vote for Gandhi was illuminated by the cries of the crowd: not only "Long live Indira," but also "Long live Jawaharlal."

Isabel Perón of Argentina held elected political position in her own right prior to ascendancy to the paramount office. Elected vice-president to her husband Juan Perón's president, she succeeded him as president upon his death in 1974. Without her husband's support, one would not have expected Isabel Perón to have been elected vice-president of Argentina. Possessing only a sixth-grade education and political experience limited to that of the wife of a prominent national leader, Isabel Perón was an unlikely candidate for the presidency of one of the largest countries in South America. That she was the symbolic leader of the Perónist party until 1985 speaks more to her political abilities after her short presidency (1974–1976) than before. But pathway to political power is the theme of this section, not exercise of power. How women and men use leadership positions—their similarities and differences—waits another book.

The former prime minister of Turkey, Tansu Çiller, deserves note at this point, for she is an anomaly in the line of women leaders documented above. An American-trained economics professor, Çiller entered politics in 1990. Her family has no history of involvement in politics. Çiller, who served as economics minister prior to her election as prime minister, represented a new kind of leader in a rapidly modernizing country. She was able to bring vision and experience to the position, yet faced considerable problems dealing with what is considered Turkey's most serious immediate problem: the economy.

To summarize, these twelve leaders have established once and for all that women are fully capable of the highest achievement at the national level. Although some came from political families, they have nonetheless exploded the myth of male dominance in political leadership.

SUBNATIONAL (COMMUNITY) LEADERS

Throughout the world, women are engaged in community leadership in a variety of capacities. We focus on two rather obscure cases: Aziza Hussein of Egypt and Hasina Khan of Bangladesh (see Levy 1988). Their work involves issues most clearly associated with women and children and can be considered absolutely basic to increasing the standard of living and quality of life in any country. Each woman leads in areas of community development and women's lives that require considerable courage. Both women have exercised important leadership positions in countries that traditionally have not expected women to serve in those roles. Each took up her leadership task with women and children in local communities, and each has made a difference.

Aziza Hussein of Egypt began her career in community involvement in the 1950s. Although from a wealthy family and married to a man who became the Minister of Social Affairs, Aziza Hussein made her own unique and individual contributions to advancing the cause of women. Working with village women, she became convinced that childbearing at a very young maternal age and childbearing too frequently jeopardize the lives of both mothers and their children. For decades, Hussein pioneered the introduction of effective family planning in Egypt, remaining all the while a volunteer who gave tirelessly of her own talents to lead a movement dedicated to saving the lives of women and children. Some of the consequences of her work include changes in Egyptian law that further secure the rights of women. While she rose to prominence as president of the International Planned Parenthood Federation, her life is evidence of the leadership role that women can play at the community level.

Educated at Dhaka University in Bangladesh, Hasina Khan also exemplifies leadership in the area of community. Instrumental in developing women's programs in Bangladesh first at the village level, Hasina Khan was the first women's program officer in Bangladesh for the Save the Children foundation. Working to assuage the problems of women and children that had in part resulted from the war with India in the early 1970s, she helped expand women's programs to numerous villages through Save the Children. That work greatly expanded opportunities for women to earn income by small-scale agriculture and small businesses that can be conducted within the household, to organize savings societies that allowed women to pool their resources for the future, and to provide opportunities for literacy training and health-related matters. By the time she left the foundation in the mid-eighties, Khan's work had changed the lives of thousands of women and children.

SUMMARY

When most of us think of leadership, we think first in terms of political leadership, and then of political leadership at the national level. Opportunities for women in these positions are available, but very few women have become national political leaders. And of those women who have, still fewer have done so without the mantle of a political father or husband being placed around their shoulders. The route to leadership through supranational organization is open to some women, and those who achieve this leadership should be recognized for the contributions they make to the durability and continuity of their societies and polities. While supranational leadership is not open to all of us, each of us has opportunities for leadership within our communities, with neither title nor trappings of conventionally recognized leaders. It is in those areas of interest to women and children that major contributions for the advancement of society can be made, and, as the diligent work of Aziza Hussein and Hasina Khan has shown, the lives of women and children enhanced.

Hurdles remain to be overcome, to be sure; the glass ceiling is firmly in place, and it will be decades or epochs before women everywhere attain genuine equality of opportunity. Nonetheless, leadership roles at various levels are open to women who possess the necessary ambition, energy, determination, and skill.

CHAPTER 8

Leaders and Leadership: Research Frontiers

In the foregoing chapters we have identified, explicitly or implicitly, a series of gaps or lacunae in the study of leaders and leadership. In this chapter we will recapitulate some old lacunae and introduce some new ones.

CONCEPTS OF LEADERSHIP

Astonishing as it may be, we have seen that there is no universally agreed-upon definition of leadership, each of the many definitions having both strong and weak points. Insofar as all leadership entails leader-follower interaction, it is as imperative to study the psychology and motivation of the followers as those of the leaders. It is easier—and perhaps more rewarding and gratifying—to study the leaders who are in the limelight. Followers are elusive, hard to pin down, and too large in number for effective study. As a result, while studies of leaders abound, studies of followers are few and far between.

In our previous studies of leaders (Rejai and Phillips 1988, 1996), we have developed and applied an interactional theory of leadership— stressing the interplay between sociodemographic variables, psychological dynamics, and situational forces. While this approach has proved satisfactory for the study of political and military leaders, we doubt that it is of universal applicability.

Given these constraints, perhaps we would do well to agree on a working conception of leadership along the lines suggested in Chapter 1. Accordingly, leadership consists of life experiences and life chances whereby an individual develops a goal or a vision, has the skill to articulate that goal or vision, is capable of organizing and mobilizing human and material resources toward the realization of that goal or vision, and is able to respond to both his or her needs and those of the followers.

The great virtues of this conception are that it is broad and value-neutral and that it seems to apply to all leadership situations. On the other hand, as we concluded in Chapter 1, perhaps a single, universal definition of leadership is simply infeasible. Perhaps there are as many definitions of leadership as there are fields of human endeavor and corresponding leadership styles. Perhaps in any universal sense leadership is unknowable. These are limitations which we must simply accept and around which we must continue our work.

TYPES OF LEADERS

In all the natural and social sciences, a satisfactory typology or classification depends upon an agreed-upon definition of the phenomenon under consideration. A satisfactory typology must be based on some strict guidelines: (1) it must rest on an explicit criterion or set of criteria; (2) it must be consistent, referring *only* to the phenomenon under consideration; (3) it must be logically exhaustive, leaving nothing out; and (4) it must be "neat," with no overlaps between the types. These guidelines are not easy to adhere to, and even in the natural sciences there are occasional exceptions. An example is Euglena: a one-celled creature that has chlorophyll like a plant but moves and eats food like an animal.

In leadership studies, problems of typology construction are compounded, since we have no universally agreed-upon definition of the phenomenon under consideration. Should we agree on the working definition of leadership offered in the previous section, then the typology suggested in Chapter 3 becomes fairly feasible. To reiterate, in that chapter we adapted Burns's (1978) classification to distinguish between transforming leaders (charismatic, revolutionary, and entrepreneurial), transactional leaders (loyalist, symbolic, and manufactured), and military leaders (who, depending on circumstances, can be either transforming or transactional).

WOMEN LEADERS

As women assume greater and more prominent positions of leadership in the coming decades, studies of women leaders will become an urgent necessity. Of particular interest are the sociodemographic traits of women leaders, the psychological dynamics that propel them toward leadership roles, and the situational forces that impede or facilitate their assent. We also need systematic investigations of gender differences in leadership.

The remaining topics covered in this book are much less controversial. Motivations, functions, and differences of leaders have been investigated in much detail; however, this is not to say that the last word has been spoken in each case or that each topic does not need further research and study.

We now turn to other lacunae not mentioned in this work.

LEADERS AND ELITES

Throughout this book we have used the words "leaders" and "elites" interchangeably. There is in fact a distinction. As Searing (1969), Wiatr (1973), and Welsh (1979) have pointed out, there is a disjunction between leadership studies and elite studies: the former are particularistic, idiosyncratic, and focus upon single individuals; the latter are empirical, comparative, and focus upon collectivities. As Welsh (1979) indicates, this disjunction should be resolved by studying elites as an aspect of the general phenomenon of leadership. We have endeavored to incorporate the two in our earlier studies of leaders (see Rejai and Phillips 1979, 1983, 1988, 1996).

MINORITY AND THIRD WORLD LEADERS

As a glance at the Bibliography will demonstrate, studies of minority leaders (Native Americans, African-Americans, Hispanic-Americans, Asian-Americans) are nonexistent, and studies of Asian, African, and Latin American leaders are extremely rare. These are two areas in which further research should systematically concentrate.

CRISIS LEADERSHIP

A few studies (e.g., Leighton 1950, Hamlin 1958, Wolfenstein 1967, Janis 1982, Wiegele et al. 1985) have addressed the subject of crisis leadership. However, this area is in urgent need of further investigation. We need to know the physiological, psychological, emotional, and motivational changes that leaders experience in stress situations and how these changes affect their behavior and decisions. The central problem—and the main reason for lack of research in this area—is access to leaders in crisis situations.

TENURE OF LEADERS

Blondel (1980) studied leadership termination for leaders of government in the postwar period. He found that the tenure of leaders comes to an end because of the following circumstances: (1) medical departure: death, illness, physical exhaustion, and old age; (2) regular departure: institutionalized end of term of office, completion of a special task; and (3) irregular departure: election defeat, dismissal by parliaments or parties, coups d'etat, and dismissal by the military.

Blondel (1985) studied tenure termination for government ministers in the contemporary world. He found that the heaviest influence on ministerial duration is the type and predictability of leaders under whom ministers serve. Beyond this, he found tenure termination to be relatively short (one to five years) under the following systems: competitive prime ministerial regimes, weak monarchies, constitutional presidencies, and military regimes. By contrast, he found tenure termination to be relatively long (five years or longer) under the following systems: communist regimes, strong monarchies, and stable "charismatic" presidencies.

Bienen and van de Walle (1991) studied thousands leaders who were in power throughout the world in the nineteenth and twentieth centuries. The authors' sole focus was leader longevity or tenure in power (or, conversely, the risk of losing power). Bienen and van de Walle spent an entire book to establish what one knows intuitively—namely, that access to political power makes power seeking easier and more durable. Herewith a sample of their conclusions:

> The length of time that a leader has been in power is a very good predictor of how long that leader will continue to hold power. Even very old leaders who have been in power for long times have low risks of being replaced. . . . However, when we systematically analyze a sample of 2,256 leaders from 167 countries to ascertain their durability we find that risks fall the longer one stays. . . .
>
> Once leaders are in place, they are difficult to remove. We have noted that there are problems in distinguishing whether this is because skills are learned over time, networks are put in place, and resources are accumulated, or because less clever leaders get winnowed out earlier. We are inclined to think that leaders do learn, do build organizations of repression and collection of information, and are able to reward followers and punish opponents, rather than that a selection process among the clever and the less clever is at work. . . .
>
> Even the disadvantages of coming to power unconstitutionally seem to disappear after a few years. Unconstitutional entry into office does raise risks for leaders. Unconstitutional seizure of power is one of the most striking time-dependent variables in the study. Risks fall precipitously for unconstitutional leaders, even more precipitously than for constitutional ones, although they are higher for the former initially. (Bienen and van de Walle 1991, 98–99)

Blondel and Bienen and van de Walle notwithstanding, it is clear that tenure of leaders is a subject that needs much further study.

SUMMARY

As this book has shown, although a great deal has been accomplished in the field of leadership studies, we still have a lengthy agenda before us. The student of leaders and leadership will never be at a loss for further investigation and research. At times the task is daunting, to be sure, but given skill and perseverance, we are sure to make significant strides.

Selected Bibliography

CHAPTER 1. CONCEPTS OF LEADERSHIP

Abel, Theodore. [1938] 1965. *The Nazi Movement: Why Hitler Came to Power*. New York: Atherton Press.

Bailey, F. G. 1988. *Humbuggery and Manipulation: The Art of Leadership*. Ithaca: Cornell University Press.

Barber, James David. 1965. *The Lawmakers: Recruitment and Adaptation to Legislative Life*. New Haven: Yale University Press.

Bass, Bernard. 1981. *Stogdill's Handbook of Leadership*. New York: Free Press.

Bell, Wendell, et al. 1961. *Public Leadership*. San Francisco: Chandler.

Bennis, Warren G. 1959. "Leadership Theory and Administrative Behavior: The Problem of Authority." *Administrative Science Quarterly* 4: 259–301.

Bennis, Warren G., and Burt Nanus. 1985. *Leaders: Strategies for Taking Charge*. New York: Harper & Row.

Blondel, Jean. 1987. *Political Leadership*. Newbury Park, CA: Sage.

Blumberg, Arnold, ed. 1995. *Great Leaders, Great Tyrants? Contemporary Views of World Rulers Who Made History.* Westport, CT: Greenwood Press.

Burns, James MacGregor. 1978. *Leadership.* New York: Harper & Row.

Burton, Michael G., and John Higley. 1987. "Invitation to Elite Theory: The Basic Contentions Reconsidered." In *Power Elites and Organizations*, ed. G. William Domhoff and Thomas R. Dye. Newbury Park, CA: Sage.

Chemers, Martin M., and Roya Ayman, eds. 1993. *Leadership Theory and Research: Perspectives and Directions.* New York: Academic Press.

Clark, Kenneth E., and Miriam B. Clark. 1994. *Choosing to Lead.* Greensboro, NC: Leadership Press.

Crook, John H. 1986. "The Evolution of Leadership: A Preliminary Skirmish." In *Changing Conceptions of Leadership*, ed. Carl F. Graumann and Serge Moscovici. New York: Springer-Verlag.

Dahl, Robert A. 1958. "A Critique of the Ruling Elite Model." *American Political Science Review* 52: 463–69.

Dahl, Robert A. 1961. *Who Governs? Democracy and Power in an American City.* New Haven: Yale University Press.

Domhoff, G. William, and Thomas R. Dye, eds. 1987. *Power Elites and Organizations.* Newbury Park, CA: Sage.

Fiedler, Fred E. 1964. "A Contingency Model of Leadership Effectiveness." In *Advances in Experimental Social Psychology*, I, ed. Leonard Berkowitz. New York: Academic Press.

Fiedler, Fred E. 1967. *A Theory of Leadership Effectiveness.* New York: McGraw-Hill.

Fiedler, Fred E., and Joseph E. Garcia. 1987. *New Approaches to Effective Leadership: Cognitive Resources and Organizational Performance.* New York: Wiley.

Field, G. Lowell, and John Higley. 1980. *Elitism.* Boston: Routledge & Kegan Paul.

French, J. R. P., Jr., and B. Raven. 1959. "The Bases of Social Power." In *Studies in Social Power,* ed. Dorwin Cartwright. Ann Arbor: University of Michigan Press.

Freud, Sigmund. [1921] 1960. *Group Psychology and the Analysis of the Ego.* New York: Bantam Books.

Gardner, Howard. 1995. *Leading Minds: An Anatomy of Leadership.* New York: Basic Books.

Gardner, John W. 1986. *Leadership and Power.* Washington, DC: Independent Sector.

Gardner, John W. 1986. *The Nature of Leadership.* Washington, DC: Independent Sector.

Gardner, John W. 1990. *On Leadership.* New York: Free Press.

George, Alexander L. 1968. "Power as a Compensatory Value for Political Leaders." *Journal of Social Issues* 3: 29–49.

Gibb, Cecil A. 1958. "An Interactional View of the Emergence of Leadership." *Australian Journal of Psychology* 10: 101–10.

Gibb, Cecil A. 1969. "Leadership." In *Handbook of Social Psychology,* IV, ed. Gardner Linzey and Elliot Aronson. Reading, MA: Addison-Wesley.

Graumann, Carl F., and Serge Moscovici, eds. 1986. *Changing Conceptions of Leadership.* New York: Springer-Verlag.

Greenleaf, Robert K. 1977. *Servant Leadership.* New York: Paulist Press.

Gurr, Ted Robert. 1970. *Why Men Rebel.* Princeton: Princeton University Press.

Heifetz, Ronald A. 1994. *Leadership Without Easy Answers*. Cambridge: Harvard University Press.

Heifetz, Ronald L., and Riley M. Sinder. 1987. "Political Leadership: Managing the Public's Problem Solving." In *The Power of Public Ideas*, ed. Robert B. Reich. Cambridge, MA: Ballinger.

Hermann, Margaret G., ed. 1977. *A Psychological Examination of Political Leaders*. New York: Free Press.

Hermann, Margaret G. 1986. "Ingredients of Leadership." In *Political Psychology*, ed. Margaret G. Hermann. San Francisco: Jossey-Bass.

Hersey, Paul. 1984. *The Situational Leader*. New York: Warner Books.

Hertz, Rosanna, and Jonathan B. Imber. 1995. *Studying Elites Using Qualitative Methods*. Thousand Oaks, CA: Sage Publications.

Hodgkinson, Christopher. 1983. *The Philosophy of Leadership*. New York: St. Martin's Press.

Hoerder, Dirk. 1977. *Crowd Action in Revolutionary Massachusetts, 1765–1780*. New York: Academic Press.

Hollander, Edwin P. 1978. *Leadership Dynamics*. New York: Free Press.

Hollander, Edwin P., and J. W. Julian. 1968. "Leadership." In *Handbook of Personality Theory and Research*, ed. Edgar P. Borgatta and W. W. Lambert. Chicago: Rand McNally.

Hook, Sidney. 1943. *The Hero in History*. Boston: Beacon Press.

House, Robert J. 1971. "A Path Goal Theory of Leadership Effectiveness." *Administrative Science Quarterly* 16: 321–38.

Hunter, Floyd. 1953. *Community Power Structure*. Chapel Hill: University of North Carolina Press.

Iremonger, Lucille. 1970. *The Fiery Chariot: A Study of the British Prime Ministers and the Search for Love.* London: Secker & Warburg.

Janda, Kenneth. 1960. "Toward the Explication of the Concept of Leadership in Terms of the Concept of Power." *Human Relations* 30: 345–63.

Kanungo, Rabindra N., and Manuel Mendonca. 1995. *Ethical Dimensions of Leadership.* Thousand Oaks, CA: Sage Publications

Kavanaugh, Dennis. 1980. "Political Leadership: The Labors of Sisyphus." In *Challenge to Governance: Studies in Overload Politics*, ed. Richard Rose. Beverly Hills, CA: Sage.

Kellerman, Barbara, ed. 1984. *Leadership: Multidisciplinary Perspectives.* Englewood Cliffs, NJ: Prentice-Hall.

Kellerman, Barbara, ed. 1986. *Political Leadership: A Source Book.* Pittsburgh: University of Pittsburgh Press.

Korten, D. C. 1962. "Situational Determinants of Leadership Structure." *Journal of Conflict Resolution* 6: 222–35.

Kouzes, James M., and Barry Z. Posner. 1995. *The Leadership Challenge: How to Keep Getting Extraordinary Things Done in Organizations.* San Francisco: Jossey-Bass.

Lasswell, Harold D. [1930] 1960. *Psychopathology and Politics.* New York: Viking Press.

Le Bon, Gustave. 1908. *The Crowd: A Study of Popular Mind.* London: Allen & Unwin.

Locke, Edwin A., et al. 1991. *The Essence of Leadership: The Four Keys to Leading Successfully.* New York: Lexington Books.

Lombardo, Michael M. 1978. *Looking at Leadership: Some Neglected Issues.* Greensboro, NC: Center for Creative Leadership.

Mann, Alistair. 1985. *Leaders We Deserve.* London: Blackwell.

McCall, Morgan W., Jr. 1977. *Leaders and Leadership: Of Substance and Shadow.* Greensboro, NC: Center for Creative Leadership.

McCall, Morgan W., Jr. 1978. *Leadership as a Design Problem.* Greensboro, NC: Center for Creative Leadership.

McCall, Morgan W., Jr., and Michael M. Lombardo, eds. 1978. *Leadership: Where Else Can We Go?* Durham: Duke University Press.

Meindl, James R., Sanford B. Ehrich, and Janet M. Eukerich. 1985. "The Romance of Leadership." *Administrative Science Quarterly* 30: 78–102.

Meisel, James H. 1958. *The Myth of the Ruling Class.* Ann Arbor: University of Michigan Press.

Michels, Robert. [1915] 1962. *Political Parties: A Sociological Study of the Oligarchical Tendencies of Modern Democracy.* New York: Collier Books.

Mills, C. Wright. 1956. *The Power Elite.* New York: Oxford University Press.

Mosca, Gaetano. 1939. *The Ruling Class.* New York: McGraw-Hill.

Mosca, Gaetano. 1958. "The Final Version of the Theory of the Ruling Class." In *The Myth of the Ruling Class,* James H. Meisel. Ann Arbor: University of Michigan Press.

Mumford, Eben. 1909. *The Origins of Leadership.* Chicago: University of Chicago Press.

Ogburn, William F. 1926. "The Great Man Versus Social Forces." *Social Forces* 5: 225–31.

Paige, Glenn D., ed. 1972. *Political Leadership*. New York: Free Press.

Paige, Glenn D. 1977. *The Scientific Study of Political Leadership*. New York: Free Press.

Pareto, Vilfredo. 1935. *The Mind and Society*. 4 vols. London: Jonathan Cape.

Pareto, Vilfredo. 1968. *The Rise and Fall of the Elites*. Totowa, NJ: Bedminister Press.

Payne, James L., et al. 1984. *The Motivations of Politicians*. Chicago: Nelson-Hall.

Pfeffer, Jeffrey. 1978. "The Ambiguity of Leadership." In *Leadership: Where Else Can We Go?* ed. Morgan W. McCall, Jr., and Michael M. Lombardo. Durham: Duke University Press.

Pigors, Paul. 1935. *Leadership or Domination*. Boston: Houghton Mifflin.

Rejai, Mostafa, and Kay Phillips. 1979. *Leaders of Revolution*. Beverly Hills, CA: Sage.

Rejai, Mostafa, and Kay Phillips. 1983. *World Revolutionary Leaders*. New Brunswick: Rutgers University Press.

Rejai, Mostafa, and Kay Phillips. 1988. *Loyalists and Revolutionaries: Political Leaders Compared*. New York: Praeger.

Rejai, Mostafa, and Kay Phillips. 1996. *World Military Leaders*. Westport, CT: Praeger.

Rosenbach, William E., and Robert L. Taylor, eds. 1984. *Contemporary Issues in Leadership*. Boulder, CO: Westview Press.

Rost, Joseph D. 1993. *Leadership for the Twenty-First Century*. Westport, CT: Praeger.

Rudé, George. 1959. *The Crowd in the French Revolution*. Oxford: Oxford University Press.

Rudé, George. 1964. *The Crowd in History: A Study of Popular Disturbances in France and England, 1730–1848*. New York: Wiley.

Rustow, Dankwart A., ed. 1970. *Philosophers and Kings: Studies in Leadership*. New York: Braziller.

Searing, Donald. 1969. "Models and Images of Man and Society in Leadership Theory." *Journal of Politics* 31: 3–31.

Selznick, Phillip. 1957. *Leadership in Administration*. Evanston, IL: Row, Peterson & Co.

Soloway, Scott M. 1987. "Elite Cohesion in Dahl's New Haven: Three Centuries of the Private School." In *Power Elites and Organizations*, ed. G. William Domhoff and Thomas R. Dye. Newbury Park, CA: Sage.

Stogdill, Ralph M. [1948] 1974. "Leadership Traits: 1904–1947." *Handbook of Leadership*. New York: Free Press.

Tucker, Robert C. 1981. *Politics as Leadership*. Columbia, MO: University of Missouri Press.

Welsh, William A. 1979. *Leaders and Elites*. New York: Holt, Rinehart & Winston.

Willhoite, Fred H., Jr. 1976. "Primates and Political Authority: A Biobehavioral Perspective." *American Political Science Review* 70: 110–26.

Willner, Ann Ruth. 1984. *The Spellbinders: Charismatic Political Leadership*. New Haven: Yale University Press.

Wills, Garry. 1994. *Certain Trumpets: The Call of Leaders*. New York: Simon & Schuster.

Winter, David G. 1973. *The Power Motive*. New York: Free Press.

Yukl, Bary A. 1981. *Leadership in Organization*. Englewood Cliffs, NJ: Prentice-Hall.

Zaleznik, Abraham. 1977. "Managers and Leaders: Are They Different?" *Harvard Business Review* 55: 67–78.

CHAPTER 2. LEADERS, FOLLOWERS, AND SKILLS

Abel, Theodore. [1938] 1965. *The Nazi Movement: Why Hitler Came to Power*. New York: Atherton Press.

Adorno, T. W., et al. 1950. *The Authoritarian Personality*. New York: Harper & Bros.

Bennis, Warren G., and Burt Nanus. 1985. *Leaders: Strategies for Taking Charge*. New York: Harper & Row.

Brinton, Crane. 1930. *The Jacobins: An Essay in the New History*. New York: Macmillan.

Flanagan, John C. 1961. "Leadership Skills: Their Identification, Development, and Evaluation." In *Leadership and Interpersonal Behavior*, ed. Luigi Petrullo and Bernard M. Bass. New York: Holt, Rinehart & Winston.

Freud, Sigmund. [1921] 1960. *Group Psychology and the Analysis of the Ego*. New York: Bantam Books.

Freud, Sigmund. 1939. *Moses and Monotheism*. New York: Kroft.

Fromm, Eric. 1941. *Escape from Freedom*. New York: Holt.

Gardner, John W. 1986. *The Heart of the Matter: Leader-Constituent Interaction*. Washington, DC: Independent Sector.

Hoerder, Dirk. 1977. *Crowd Action in Revolutionary Massachusetts, 1765–1780*. New York: Academic Press.

Hoffer, Eric. 1958. *The True Believer*. New York: New American Library.

Huntington, Samuel P. 1968. *Political Order in Changing Societies*. New Haven: Yale University Press.

Janis, Irving L. 1982. *Groupthink*. Boston: Houghton Mifflin.

Kellerman, Barbara, ed. 1986. *Political Leadership: A Source Book.* Pittsburgh: University of Pittsburgh Press.

Le Bon, Gustave. 1908. *The Crowd: A Study of Popular Mind.* London: Allen & Unwin.

Le Bon, Gustave. 1913. *The Psychology of Revolution.* New York: Putnam.

Lenin, V. I. [1902] 1943. *What Is To Be Done?* New York: International Publishers.

Mazlish, Bruce. 1981. "The Leader and Led, Individual and Group." *Psychohistory Review* 9: 218–28.

Merkl, Peter. 1975. *Political Violence Under the Swastika.* Princeton: Princeton University Press.

Merkl, Peter. 1981. *The Making of a Stormtrooper.* Princeton: Princeton University Press.

Michels, Robert. [1915] 1962. *Political Parties: A Sociological Study of the Oligarchical Tendencies of Modern Democracy.* New York: Collier Books.

Milgram, Stanley. 1974. *Obedience to Authority.* New York: Harper & Row.

Rosenbach, William E., and Robert L. Taylor, eds. 1984. *Contemporary Issues in Leadership.* Boulder, CO: Westview Press.

Rudé, George. 1959. *The Crowd in the French Revolution.* Oxford: Oxford University Press.

Rudé, George. 1964. *The Crowd in History: A Study of Popular Disturbances in France and England, 1730–1848.* New York: Wiley.

Selznick, Philip. 1952. *The Organizational Weapon.* New York: McGraw-Hill.

Stephenson, T. E. 1959. "The Leader-Follower Relationship." *Sociological Review* 7: 179–95.

Suedfeld, Peter, and A. D. Rank. 1976. "Revolutionary Leaders: Long-Term Success as a Function of Changes in Conceptual Complexity." *Journal of Personality and Social Psychology* 34: 169–78.

Uldricks, Teddy J. 1974. "The 'Crowd' in the Russian Revolution: Toward Reassessing the Nature of Revolutionary Leadership." *Politics and Society* 4: 397–413.

Wills, Garry. 1994. *Certain Trumpets: The Call of Leaders*. New York: Simon & Schuster.

Zimbardo, Philip G., et al. 1973. "A Pirandellian Prison." *New York Times Magazine*, 8 April: 38–39+.

CHAPTER 3. TYPES OF LEADERS

Arendt, Hannah. 1968. *Totalitarianism*. New York: Harcourt Brace & World.

Barber, James David. 1965. *The Lawmakers: Recruitment and Adaptation to Legislative Life*. New Haven: Yale University Press.

Bass, Bernard. 1981. *Stogdill's Handbook of Leadership*. New York: Free Press.

Bensman, J., and M. Givant. 1975. "Charisma and Modernity: The Use and Abuse of a Concept." *Social Research* 42: 570–614.

Brinton, Crane. 1930. *The Jacobins: An Essay in the New History*. New York: Macmillan.

Brinton, Crane. 1965. *Anatomy of Revolution*. New York: Vantage Books.

Brown, William B. 1960. *The People's Choice: Presidential Image in Campaign Biography*. Baton Rouge: Louisiana State University Press.

Burns, James MacGregor. 1978. *Leadership*. New York: Harper & Row.

Clark, Kenneth E., and Miriam B. Clark. 1994. *Choosing to Lead*. Greensboro, NC: Leadership Press.

Downton, James V. 1973. *Rebel Leadership: Commitment and Charisma in the Revolutionary Process*. New York: Free Press.

Edelman, Murray. 1964. *The Symbolic Uses of Politics*. Urbana: University of Illinois Press.

Edelman, Murray. 1971. *Politics as Symbolic Action*. New York: Academic Press.

Elder, Charles D., and Roger W. Cobb. 1983. *The Political Uses of Symbols*. New York: Longman.

Germino, Dante L. 1959. *The Italian Fascist Party in Power*. Minneapolis: University of Minnesota Press.

Gerth, Hans. 1940. "The Nazi Party: Its Leadership and Composition." *American Journal of Sociology* 45: 517–41.

Gilbert, G. M. 1950. *Psychology of Dictatorship: Based on an Examination of Leaders of Nazi Germany*. New York: Ronald Press.

Glassman, Ronald. 1975. "Legitimacy and Manufactured Charisma." *Social Research* 42: 615–36.

Good, William J. 1978. *The Celebration of Heroes: Prestige as a Social Control System*. Berkeley: University of California Press.

Gouldner, Alvin W., ed. 1950. *Studies in Leadership*. New York: Harper & Row.

Hoffer, Eric. 1958. *The True Believer*. New York: New American Library.

Inkeles, Alex. 1961. "National Character and Modern Political Systems." In *Psychological Anthropology*, ed. Francis L. K. Hsu. Homewood, IL: Dorsey Press.

Kellerman, Barbara, ed. 1986. *Political Leadership: A Source Book*. Pittsburgh: University of Pittsburgh Press.

Kennan, Nadav, and Martha Hadley. 1986. "The Creation of Political Leaders in the Context of American Politics of the 1970s and the 1980s." In *Changing Concepts of*

Leadership, ed. Carl F. Graumann and Serge Moscovici. New York: Springer-Verlag.

Klapp, Orrin R. 1948. "The Creation of Popular Heroes." *American Journal of Sociology* 54: 135–41.

Klapp, Orrin R. 1964. *Symbolic Leaders: Public Dramas and Public Men*. Chicago: Aldine.

Korten, D. C. 1962. "Situational Determinants of Leadership Structure." *Journal of Conflict Resolution* 6: 222–35.

Lasswell, Harold D. [1948] 1962. *Power and Personality*. New York: Viking.

Lasswell, Harold D. 1951. "The Democratic Character." In *The Political Writings of Harold D. Lasswell*. New York: Free Press.

Lasswell, Harold D., and Daniel Lerner, eds. 1965. *World Revolutionary Elites*. Cambridge: MIT Press.

Leighton, A. H. 1950. "Leadership in a Stress Situation." In *Studies in Leadership*, ed. Alvin W. Gouldner. New York: Harper & Bros.

Lewin, R. Lippitt, and R. K. White. 1939. "Patterns of Aggressive Behavior in Experimentally Created Social Climates." *Journal of Social Psychology* 10: 271–99.

Lewis, Eugene. 1980. *Public Entrepreneurship*. Bloomington: Indiana University Press.

Linton, Ralph. 1951. "The Concept of National Character." In *Personality and Political Crisis*, ed. Alfred H. Stanton and Stewart E. Perry. New York: Free Press.

Martin, James K. 1973. *Men in Rebellion*. New Brunswick: Rutgers University Press.

Neumann, Sigmund. 1941. "Leadership: Institutional and Personal." *Journal of Politics* 3: 133–53.

Ratnam, K. J. 1964. "Charisma and Political Leadership." *Political Studies* 12: 341–54.

Rejai, Mostafa, and Kay Phillips. 1979. *Leaders of Revolution*. Beverly Hills, CA: Sage.

Rejai, Mostafa, and Kay Phillips. 1983. *World Revolutionary Leaders*. New Brunswick: Rutgers University Press.

Rejai, Mostafa, and Kay Phillips. 1988. *Loyalists and Revolutionaries: Political Leaders Compared*. New York: Praeger.

Rejai, Mostafa, and Kay Phillips. 1996. *World Military Leaders*. Westport, CT: Praeger.

Rustow, Dankwart A., ed. 1970. *Philosophers and Kings: Studies in Leadership*. New York: Braziller.

Schneider, Mark, and Paul Teske, with Michael Mintrom. 1995. *Public Entrepreneurs: Agents for Change in American Government*. Princeton: Princeton University Press.

Schweitzer, Arthur. 1984. *The Age of Charisma*. Chicago: Nelson-Hall.

Stewart, D., and T. Hoult. 1959. "A Social-Psychological Theory of the Authoritarian Personality." *American Journal of Sociology* 65: 274–79.

Tucker, Robert C. 1965. "The Dictator and Totalitarianism." *World Politics* 17: 565–73.

Tucker, Robert C. 1968. "The Theory of Charismatic Leadership." *Daedalus* 97: 731–56.

Tucker, Robert C. 1981. *Politics as Leadership*. Columbia, MO: University of Missouri Press.

Weber, Max. 1958. *From Max Weber: Essays in Sociology*. Ed. H. H. Gerth and C. Wright Mills. New York: Oxford University Press.

Weber, Max. 1964. *The Theory of Social and Economic Organization*. Ed. Talcott Parsons. New York: Free Press.

Willner, Ann Ruth. 1984. *The Spellbinders: Charismatic Political Leadership*. New Haven: Yale University Press.

CHAPTER 4. MOTIVATIONS OF LEADERS

Adler, Alfred. [1928] 1966. "The Psychology of Power." *Journal of Individual Psychology* 22: 166–72.

Albin, Mel, et al., eds. 1980. *New Directions in Psychohistory*. Lexington, MA: Lexington Books.

Avner, Falk. 1985. "Aspects of Psychobiography." *Political Psychology* 6: 605–20.

Barber, James David. 1965. *The Lawmakers: Recruitment and Adaptation to Legislative Life*. New Haven: Yale University Press.

Blanchard, William B. 1984. *Revolutionary Morality*. Santa Barbara. CA: ABC-Clio.

Browning, Rufus P., and Herbert Jacob. 1964. "Power Motivation and the Political Personality." *Public Opinion Quarterly* 28: 75–90.

Coles, Robert H. 1970. *Erik H. Erikson: The Growth of His Thought*. Boston: Little, Brown.

Crosby, Faye. 1979. "Evaluating Psychohistorical Explanations." *The Psycho-History Review* 7: 6–16.

Crosby, Faye, and Travis L. Crosby. 1981. "Psychobiography and Psychohistory." In *Handbook of Political Behavior*, I, ed. Samuel Long. New York: Plenum Press.

Erikson, Erik H. [1942] 1963. "The Legend of Hitler's Youth." In *Childhood and Society*. 2nd ed. New York: Norton.

Erikson, Erik H. 1962. *Young Man Luther: A Study in Psychoanalysis and History*. New York: Norton.

Erikson, Erik H. 1963. *Childhood and Society*. 2nd ed. New York: Norton.

Erikson, Erik H. 1969. *Gandhi's Truth: On the Origins of Militant Nonviolence*. New York: Norton.

Freud, Sigmund. [1921] 1960. *Group Psychology and the Analysis of the Ego*. New York: Bantam Books.

Freud, Sigmund. 1939. *Moses and Monotheism*. New York: Knopf.

George, Alexander L. 1968. "Power as a Compensatory Value for Political Leaders." *Journal of Social Issues* 3: 29–49.

Glad, Betty. 1973. "Contributions of Psychobiography." In *Handbook of Political Psychology*, ed. Jean N. Knutson. San Francisco: Jossey-Bass.

Iremonger, Lucille. 1970. *The Fiery Chariot: A Study of the British Prime Ministers and the Search for Love*. London: Secker & Warburg.

Kellerman, Barbara, ed. 1986. *Political Leadership: A Source Book*. Pittsburgh: University of Pittsburgh Press.

Lasswell, Harold D. [1930] 1960. *Psychopathology and Politics*. New York: Viking Press.

Lasswell, Harold D. [1948] 1962. *Power and Personality*. New York: Free Press.

Madsen, Douglas. 1985. "A Biochemical Property Relating to Power Seeking in Humans." *American Political Science Review* 79: 448–57.

Madsen, Douglas. 1986. "Power Seekers Are Different: Further Biochemical Evidence." *American Political Science Review* 80: 261–70.

Matthews, Donald R. 1960. *U.S. Senators and Their World*. Chapel Hill: University of North Carolina Press.

Mazlish, Bruce. 1976. *The Revolutionary Ascetic*. New York: Basic Books.

McClelland, David C. 1961. *The Achieving Society*. Princeton, NJ: Van Nostrand.

McClelland, David C. 1970. "The Two Faces of Power." *Journal of International Affairs* 24: 29–47.

McClelland, David C., et al. 1953. *The Achievement Motive*. New York: Appleton-Century-Croft.

McGregor, Douglas. 1966. *Leadership and Motivation.* Cambridge: MIT Press.

Payne, James L., et al. 1984. *The Motivation of Politicians.* Chicago: Nelson-Hall.

Rejai, Mostafa, and Kay Phillips. 1988. *Loyalists and Revolutionaries: Political Leaders Compared.* New York: Praeger.

Roazen, Paul. 1976. *Erik H. Erikson: The Power and Limits of a Vision.* New York: Free Press.

Rosenbach, William E., and Robert L. Taylor, eds. 1984. *Contemporary Issues in Leadership.* Boulder, CO: Westview Press.

Strozier, Charles B., and Daniel Offer, eds. 1985. *The Leader: Psychohistorical Essays.* New York: Plenum Press.

Winter, David G. 1973. *The Power Motive.* New York: Free Press.

Wolfenstein, E. Victor. 1967. *The Revolutionary Personality: Lenin, Trotsky, Gandhi.* Princeton: Princeton University Press.

CHAPTER 5. FUNCTIONS OF LEADERS

Barnard, Chester I. 1947. *The Functions of the Executive.* Cambridge: Harvard University Press.

Burns, James MacGregor. 1978. *Leadership.* New York: Harper & Row.

Crook, John H. 1986. "The Evolution of Leadership: A Preliminary Skirmish." In *Changing Conceptions of Leadership*, ed. F. Graumann and Serge Moscovici. New York: Springer-Verlag.

Davies, James C. 1963. *Human Nature in Politics.* New York: Wiley.

Davies, James C. 1986. "Roots of Political Behavior." In *Political Psychology*, ed. Margaret G. Hermann. San Francisco: Jossey-Bass.

Fitzgerald, Ross. 1985. "Human Needs and Politics: The Ideas of Christian Bay and Herbert Marcuse." *Political Psychology* 6: 87–108.

Gardner, John W. 1965. *The Antileadership Vaccine*. New York: Carnegie Corporation.

Gardner, John W. 1986. *The Tasks of Leadership*. Washington, DC: Independent Sector.

Hodgkinson, Christopher. 1983. *The Philosophy of Leadership*. New York: St. Martin's Press.

Katz, Elihu, and Daniel Dayan. 1986. "Contests, Conquests, and Coronations: Of Media Events and Their Heroes." In *Changing Conceptions of Leadership*, ed. Carl F. Graumann and Serge Moscovici. New York: Springer-Verlag.

Kavanaugh, Dennis. 1980. "Political Leadership: The Labors of Sisyphus." In *Challenge to Governance: Studies in Overload Politics*, ed. Richard Rose. Beverly Hills, CA: Sage.

Keller, Suzanne. 1963. *Beyond the Ruling Class: Strategic Elites in Modern Society*. New York: Random House.

Kincheloe, Samuel C. 1928. "The Prophet as a Leader." *Sociology and Social Research* 12: 461–68.

Lane, Robert E. 1978. "Interpersonal Relations and Leadership in a 'Cold Society.'" *Comparative Politics* 10: 443–59.

Maslow, Abraham. [1950] 1970. *Motivation and Personality*. Revised ed. New York: Harper & Row.

McClelland, David C. 1970. "The Two Faces of Power." *Journal of International Affairs* 24: 29–47.

Meindl, James R., Sanford B. Ehrich, and Janet M. Eukerich. 1985. "The Romance of Leadership." *Administrative Science Quarterly* 30: 78–102.

Moos, Malcolm, and Bertram Koslin. 1951. "Political Leadership Reexamined: An Experimental Approach." *Public Opinion Quarterly* 15: 463–74.

Parsons, Talcott. 1951. *The Social System.* New York: Free Press.

Rost, Joseph D. 1993. *Leadership for the Twenty-First Century.* Westport, CT: Praeger.

Shils, Edward, and Michael Young. 1953. "The Meaning of the Coronation." *Sociological Review* 1: 63–82.

Tucker, Robert C. 1965. "The Dictator and Totalitarianism." *World Politics* 17: 563–73.

Wildavsky, Aaron. 1984. *The Nursing Father: Moses as a Political Leader.* University, AL: University of Alabama Press.

Willhoite, Fred H., Jr. 1976. "Primates and Political Authority: A Biobehavioral Perspective." *American Political Science Review* 70: 110–26.

CHAPTER 6. COMPARATIVE STUDIES OF LEADERS

Aberbach, Joel D., Robert D. Putnam, and Bert A. Rockman. 1981. *Bureaucrats and Politicians in Western Democracies.* Cambridge: Harvard University Press.

Armstrong, John A. 1972. *The European Administrative Elite.* Princeton: Princeton University Press.

Beck, Carl, et al. 1973. *Comparative Communist Political Leadership.* New York: McKay.

Bell, Daniel. 1958. "The Power Elite Reconsidered." *American Journal of Sociology* 64: 238–50.

Bell, Wendell. 1964. *Jamaican Leaders: Political Attitudes in a New Nation.* Berkeley: University of California Press.

Berger, Morroe. 1957. *Bureaucracy and Society in Modern Egypt: A Study of the Higher Civil Service*. Princeton: Princeton University Press.

Blondel, Jean. 1980. *World Leaders: Heads of Government in the Postwar Period*. Beverly Hills, CA: Sage.

Blondel, Jean. 1985. *Government Ministers in the Contemporary World*. Beverly Hills, CA: Sage.

Blondel, Jean. 1987. *Political Leadership*. Newbury Park, CA: Sage.

Bonilla, Frank. 1970. *The Failure of [Venezuelan] Elites*. Cambridge: MIT Press.

Buck, Phillip W. 1963. *Amateurs and Professionals in British Politics, 1918–1959*. Chicago: University of Chicago Press.

Bunce, Valerie. 1981. *Do New Leaders Make a Difference?* Princeton: Princeton University Press.

Burton, Michael G., and John Higley. 1987. "Invitation to Elite Theory: The Basic Contentions Reconsidered" In *Power Elites and Organizations*, ed. G. William Domhoff and Thomas R. Dye. Newbury Park, CA: Sage.

Cheng, Peter. 1974. "The Japanese Cabinets, 1885–1973: An Elite Analysis." *Asian Survey* 14: 1055–71.

Cohan, A. S. 1972. *The Irish Political Elite*. Dublin: Gill and Macmillan.

Dahl, Robert A. 1958. "A Critique of the Ruling Elite Model." *American Political Science Review* 52: 463–69.

Dahl, Robert A. 1961. *Who Governs? Democracy and Power in an American City*. New Haven: Yale University Press.

Davis, Jerome. 1929. "A Study of 163 Outstanding [Russian] Communist Leaders." *American Sociological Review* 24: 42–55.

Dodd, C. H. 1964. "The Social and Educational Background of Turkish Officials." *Middle Eastern Studies* 1: 268–76.

Dogan, Mattei. 1961. "Political Ascent in a Class Society: French Deputies 1870–1958." In *Political Decision-Makers*, ed. Dwaine Marvick. New York: Free Press.

Dogan, Mattei, ed. 1975. *The Mandarins of Western Europe*. Beverly Hills, CA: Sage.

Domhoff, G. William. 1970. *The Higher Circles: The Governing Class in America*. New York: Vintage.

Domhoff, G. William. 1978. *Who Really Rules: New Haven and Community Power Reexamined*. New Brunswick, NJ: Transaction Books.

Domhoff, G. William, and Thomas R. Dye, eds. 1987. *Power Elites and Organizations*. Newbury Park, CA: Sage.

Dye, Thomas R. 1983. *Who's Running America?* Englewood Cliffs, NJ: Prentice-Hall.

Edinger, Lewis J. 1960. "Post-Totalitarian Leadership: Elites in the German Federal Republic." *American Political Science Review* 54: 58–82.

Edinger, Lewis J. 1961. "Continuity and Change in the Background of German Decision-Makers." *Western Political Quarterly* 14: 17–36.

Edinger, Lewis J., ed. 1967. *Political Leadership in Industrialized Societies*. New York: Wiley.

Edinger, Lewis J. 1975. "The Comparative Analysis of Political Leadership." *Comparative Politics* 7: 253–69.

Farrell, R. Barry, ed. 1970. *Political Leadership in Eastern Europe and Soviet Union*. Chicago: Aldine.

Fleron, Frederic J., Jr., ed. 1969. *Communist Studies and the Social Sciences*. Chicago: Rand McNally.

Frey, Frederick W. 1965. *The Turkish Political Elite*. Cambridge: MIT Press.

Guttsman, W. L. 1964. *The British Political Elite*. New York: Basic Books.

Harris, J. S., and T. V. Garcia. 1966. "The Permanent Secretaries: Britain's Top Administrators." *Public Administration Review* 26: 31–44.

Hoogenboom, Ari. 1968. "Industrialism and Political Leadership: A Case Study of the United States Senate." In *The Age of Industrialism in America*, ed. Frederick C. Jaher. New York: Free Press.

Hunter, Floyd. 1953. *Community Power Structure*. Chapel Hill: University of North Carolina Press.

Johnson, R. W. 1973. "The British Political Elite, 1955–1970." *European Journal of Sociology* 14: 35–77.

Kautsky, John H. 1969. "Revolutionary and Managerial Elites in Modernizing Regimes." *Comparative Politics* 1: 441–67.

Keller, Suzanne. 1963. *Beyond the Ruling Class: Strategic Elites in Modern Society*. New York: Random House.

Lacouture, Jean. 1970. *Demigods: Charismatic Leadership in the Third World*. New York: Knopf.

Laski, Harold J. 1928. "The Personnel of the British Cabinet, 1801–1924." *American Political Science Review* 22: 12–31.

Lasswell, Harold D., and Daniel Lerner, eds. 1965. *World Revolutionary Elites*. Cambridge: MIT Press.

Lasswell, Harold D., et al. 1952. *The Comparative Study of Elites*. Stanford: Stanford University Press.

Lee, Ming T. 1968. "The Founders of the Chinese Communist Party: A Study in Revolutionaries." *Civilisations* 13: 113–27.

Lewis, Paul A. 1972. "The Spanish Ministerial Elite, 1938–1969." *Comparative Politics* 5: 83–106.

Lewis, Paul A. 1978. "Salazar's Ministerial Elite, 1932–1968." *Journal of Politics* 40: 622–47.

Linden, Ronald H., and Bert A. Rockman, eds. 1985. *Elite Studies and Communist Politics*. Pittsburgh: University of Pittsburgh Press.

Lipset, Seymour Martin, and Aldo Solari, eds. 1973. *Elites in Latin America*. New York: Oxford University Press.

Lynd, Robert S., and Helen M. Lynd. 1929. *Middletown*. New York: Harcourt, Brace.

Lynd, Robert S., and Helen M. Lynd. 1937. *Middletown in Transition*. New York: Harcourt, Brace.

Marvick, Dwaine, ed. 1961. *Political Decision-Makers*. New York: Free Press.

Matthews, Donald R. 1954. *The Social Background of Political Decision-Makers*. New York: Doubleday.

Matthews, Donald R. 1960. *U.S. Senators and Their World*. Chapel Hill: University of North Carolina Press.

Mellors, Colin. 1978. *The British MP: A Socioeconomic Study of the House of Commons*. Westmead, Farnborough, England: Saxon House.

Mills, C. Wright. 1956. *The Power Elite*. New York: Oxford University Press.

Morris-Jones, W. H., ed. 1976. *The Making of Politicians: Studies from Africa and Asia*. University of London: Althone Press.

Parenti, Michael. 1970. "Power and Pluralism: A View from the Bottom." *Journal of Politics* 32: 501–30.

Park, Richard L., and Irene Tinker. 1959. *Leadership and Political Institutions in India*. Princeton: Princeton University Press.

Pessen, Edward. 1984. *The Log Cabin Myth: The Social Backgrounds of the Presidents*. New Haven: Yale University Press.

Polsby, Nelson. 1963. *Community Power and Political Theory*. New Haven: Yale University Press.

Putnam, Robert D. 1976. *The Comparative Study of Political Elites*. Englewood Cliffs, NJ: Prentice-Hall.

Quandt, William R. 1970. *The Comparative Study of Political Elites*. Beverly Hills, CA: Sage.

Rejai, Mostafa, and Kay Phillips. 1988. *Loyalists and Revolutionaries: Political Leaders Compared*. New York: Praeger.

Rejai, Mostafa, and Kay Phillips. 1996. *World Military Leaders*. Westport, CT: Praeger.

Rejai, Mostafa, and Kay Phillips, with Warren L. Mason. 1993. *Demythologizing an Elite: American Presidents in Empirical, Comparative, and Historical Perspective*. Westport, CT: Praeger.

Rustow, Dankwart A. 1966. "The Study of Elites: Who's Who, When, and How." *World Politics* 18: 690–717.

Rustow, Dankwart A. 1967. *A World of Nations: Problems of Political Modernization*. Washington, DC: Brookings Institution.

Scalapino, Robert A., ed. 1969. The Communist Revolution in Asia. 2nd ed. Englewood Cliffs, NJ: Prentice-Hall.

Smythe, H. H., and M. M. Smythe. 1960. *The New Nigerian Elite*. Stanford: Stanford University Press.

Soloway, Scott M. 1987. "Elite Cohesion in Dahl's New Haven: Three Centuries of the Private School." In *Power Elites and Organizations*, ed. G. William Domhoff and Thomas R. Dye. Newbury Park, CA: Sage.

Strauss, Harlan J. 1973. "Revolutionary Types: Russia in 1905." *Journal of Conflict Resolution* 17: 297–316.

Takane, Masaki. 1981. *The Political Elite in Japan*. Berkeley: University of California, Center for Japanese Studies.

Theakston, Kevin. 1987. *Junior Ministers in British Parliament*. New York: Blackwell.

Von der Mehden, Fred. 1964. *The Politics of the Developing Nations*. Englewood Cliffs, NJ: Prentice-Hall.

Wilson, Gordon. 1966. "The African Elite." In *The Transformation of East Africa*, ed. Stanley Diamond and Fred Burke. New York: Basic Books.

Winder, R. Bayly. 1962–1963. "Syrian Deputies and Cabinet Ministers, 1919–1959." Parts 1, 2. *Middle East Journal* 16: 407–27 and 17: 35–54.

Wolfinger, Raymond E. 1974. *The Politics of Progress*. Englewood Cliffs, NJ: Prentice-Hall.

Zartman, I. William. 1980. *Elites in the Middle East*. New York: Praeger.

Zonis, Marvin. 1971. *The Political Elite of Iran*. Princeton: Princeton University Press.

CHAPTER 7. WOMEN LEADERS

Apfelbaum, Erika, and Martha Hadley. 1986. "Leadership Ms.-Qualified: II. Reflections on an Initial Case Investigation of Contemporary Women Leaders." In *Changing Conceptions of Leadership*, ed. Carl F. Graumann and Serge Moscovici. New York: Springer-Verlag.

Barber, James D., and Barbara Kellerman, eds. 1986. *Women Leaders in American Politics*. Englewood Cliffs, NJ: Prentice-Hall.

Bass, Bernard. 1981. *Stogdill's Handbook of Leadership*. New York: Free Press.

Brichta, Avraham. 1974–75. "Women in the Knesset, 1949–1968." *Parliamentary Affairs* 28: 31–50.

Brown, S. M. 1979. "Male vs. Female Leaders: A Comparison of Empirical Studies." *Sex Roles* 5: 595–61.

Carrol, Susan J. 1985. *Women as Candidates in American Politics*. Bloomington: Indiana University Press.

Comstock, Alzada. 1926. "Women as Members of European Parliaments." *American Political Science Review* 20: 379–84.

Constantini, Edmund, and Kenneth H. Craik. 1972. "Women as Politicians: The Social Background, Personality, and Political Careers of Female Party Leaders." *Journal of Social Issues* 28: 217–36.

Currell, Melville E. 1974. *Political Woman*. London: Croom Helm.

Darcy, R., et al. 1987. *Women, Elections, and Representation*. New York: Longman.

Diamond, Irene. 1977. *Sex Roles in the State House*. New Haven: Yale University Press.

Dubeck, Paula J. 1987. "Women and Access to Political Office: A Comparison of Female and Male State Legislators." *The Sociological Quarterly* 17: 42–52.

Duerst-Lahti, Georgia, and Rita May Kelly, eds. 1995. *Gender Power, Leadership, and Governance*. Ann Arbor: University of Michigan Press.

Flamming, J. A., ed. 1984. *Political Women*. Beverly Hills, CA: Sage.

Genovese, Michael A., ed. 1993. *Women as National Leaders*. Newbury Park, CA: Sage.

Ghiloni, Beth W. 1987. "The Velvet Ghetto: Women, Power, and the Corporation." In *Power Elites and Organizations*, ed. G. William Domhoff and Thomas R. Dye. Newbury Park, CA: Sage.

Gilligan, Carol. 1982. *In a Different Voice: Psychological Theory and Women's Development*. Cambridge: Harvard University Press.

Heller, Trudy. 1982. *Women and Men as Leaders*. New York: Praeger.

Hollander, Edwin P., and Jan Yoder. 1984. "Some Issues in Comparing Women and Men as Leaders." In *Contemporary Issues in Leadership*, ed. William E.

Rosenbach and Robert L. Taylor. Boulder, CO: Westview Press.

Jamieson, Kathleen Hall. 1995. *Beyond the Double Bind: Women and Leadership.* New York: Oxford University Press.

Kelly, Rita Mae, and Mary Boutilier. 1978. *The Making of Political Women: A Study of Socialization and Role Conflict.* Chicago: Nelson-Hall.

Kirkpatrick, Jeane. 1974. *Political Woman.* New York: Basic Books.

Kohn, W. S. G. 1980. *Women in National Legislatures: A Comparative Study of Six Countries.* New York: Praeger.

Kruse, Lenelis, and M. Wintermantel. 1986. "Leadership Ms.-Qualified: I. The Gender Bias in Everyday and Scientific Thinking." In *Changing Conceptions of Leadership,* ed. Carl F. Graumann and Serge Moscovici. New York: Springer-Verlag.

Lapidus, Gail W. 1975. "Political Mobilization, Participation, and Leadership: Women in Soviet Politics." *Comparative Politics* 8: 90–118.

LeVeness, Frank P., and Jane P. Sweeney. 1987. *Women Leaders in Contemporary U.S. Politics.* Boulder, CO: Lynne Rienner.

Levy, Marion F. 1988. *Each in Her Own Way: Five Women Leaders of the Developing World.* Boulder, CO: Lynne Rienner.

Moore, Gwen. 1987. "Women in the Old-Boy Network: The Case of New York State Government." In *Power Elites and Organizations,* ed. G. William Domhoff and Thomas R. Dye, eds. Newbury Park, CA: Sage.

Mullaney, Marie M. 1983. *Revolutionary Women: Gender and the Socialist Revolutionary Role.* New York: Praeger.

Nelson, Barbara, and Najma Chowdhury, eds. 1994. *Women and Politics Worldwide*. New Haven: Yale University Press.

Phillips, Kay, and Mostafa Rejai. 1994. "Women as Leaders: A Research Note." *Journal of Political and Military Sociology* 22: 343–50.

Richter, L. K. 1990–1991. "Exploring Theories of Female Leadership in South and Southeast Asia." *Pacific Affairs* 6: 524–40.

Tovenski, J., and J. Hills, eds. 1984. *Women and Public Participation*. London: Routledge & Kegan Paul.

Vallance, Elizabeth, and Elizabeth Davies. 1986. *Women of Europe: Women MEPs and Social Equality*. Cambridge: Cambridge University Press.

Walsh, Elsa. 1995. *Divided Lives: The Public and Private Struggles of Three Accomplished Women*. New York: Simon & Schuster.

CHAPTER 8. LEADERS AND LEADERSHIP: RESEARCH FRONTIERS

Bass, Bernard. 1981. *Stogdill's Handbook of Leadership*. New York: Free Press.

Bienen, Henry, and Nicolas van de Walle. 1991. *Of Time and Power: Leadership Duration in the Modern World*. Stanford: Stanford University Press.

Blondel, Jean. 1980. *World Leaders: Heads of Government in the Postwar Period*. Beverly Hills, CA: Sage.

Blondel, Jean. 1985. *Government Ministers in the Contemporary World*. Beverly Hills, CA: Sage.

Burns, James MacGregor. 1978. *Leadership*. New York: Harper & Row.

Edinger, Lewis L., and Donald D. Searing. 1967. "Social Background in Elite Analysis: A Methodological

Inquiry." *American Political Science Review* 61: 428–45.

Hamlin, R. L. 1958. "Leadership and Crisis." *Sociometry* 21: 332–35.

Janis, Irving L. 1982. *Groupthink*. Boston: Houghton Mifflin.

Leighton, A. H. 1950. "Leadership in a Stress Situation." In *Studies in Leadership*, ed. Alvin W. Gouldner. New York: Harper & Bros.

Rejai, Mostafa, and Kay Phillips. 1979. *Leaders of Revolution*. Beverly Hills, CA: Sage.

Rejai, Mostafa, and Kay Phillips. 1983. *World Revolutionary Leaders*. New Brunswick: Rutgers University Press.

Rejai, Mostafa, and Kay Phillips. 1988. *Loyalists and Revolutionaries: Political Leaders Compared*. New York: Praeger.

Rejai, Mostafa, and Kay Phillips. 1996. *World Military Leaders*. Westport, CT: Praeger.

Rosenbach, William E., and Robert L. Taylor, eds. 1984. *Contemporary Issues in Leadership*. Boulder, CO: Westview Press.

Searing, Donald. 1969. "Models and Images of Man and Society in Leadership Theory." *Journal of Politics* 31: 3–31.

Welsh, William A. 1979. *Leaders and Elites*. New York: Holt, Rinehart & Winston.

Wiatr, J. 1973. "Political Elites and Political Leadership." *Indian Journal of Political Science* 17: 137–49.

Wiegele, Thomas C., et al. 1985. *Leaders Under Stress: A Psycho-Physiological Analysis of International Crisis*. Durham: Duke University Press.

Wolfenstein, E. Victor. 1967. "Some Psychological Aspects of Crisis Leaders." In *Political Leadership in Industrialized Societies*, ed. Lewis J. Edinger. New York: Wiley.

Index

About the Authors

MOSTAFA REJAI is Distinguished Professor Emeritus of Political Science at Miami University, Ohio, where he has also been the recipient of an Outstanding Teaching Award.

KAY PHILLIPS is Professor of Sociology and Anthropology at Miami University, Ohio.

Professors Rejai and Phillips are coauthors of five other books on leaders and leadership.

ISBN 0-275-95880-9

90000>

EAN

9 780275 958800

HARDCOVER BAR CODE